"If you long to be freed from the burden of living for the applause of others, read this book. In *Freedom from Performing*, Becky Harling reveals her own journey moving from perfectionism and comparison to the place of grace. She will equip you to embrace your purpose and passion while releasing the pressure of living to please others. The study guide will equip you to internalize Scripture and make choices based on transformational truth."

—CAROL KENT, speaker; author of *When I Lay My Isaac Down* and *A New Kind of Normal*

"From the opening pages of *Freedom from Performing*, author Becky Harling's words start to operate on those of us suffering with performance-driven-itis. The more we read, the more personal and intricate the surgery becomes as layers of shame and overblown self-worth are removed by the delicate scalpel of grace. Somehow Becky joins the opposites of work and rest so we performers can get things done in God's time, not ours."

—SHARON NORRIS ELLIOTT, CEO, Life That Matters Ministries; author of *Power Suit: The Armor of God Fit for the Feminine Frame*

"*Freedom from Performing* was written for all of us who are running as fast as we can and just not getting there. The race is fixed, and there's only one way to win. Author Becky Harling has nailed that truth and presents it in a clear, compelling way, inviting us to relax and rest in the fact that grace has already won and will carry us across the finish line if we'll just allow it to do so. I highly encourage every Christian who has ever entertained the thought that she is not good enough, isn't competent enough, or will never succeed to immediately stop that futile self-torture and get a copy of this book. It's the best resource on practical grace that I've seen in a very long time."

—KATHI MACIAS, award-winning author and speaker

"In a world that applauds perfection and performance, women often get lost in trying to be someone significant. This book is a treat. Tender yet firm, it helps women to a place of security in a world that breeds insecurity. I would highly recommend this as a personal and group resource for women today who eho are looking to understand of God's grace and how that grace makes a real difference."

—DEBBIE ALSDORF, author of *The Faith Dare* and The DESIGN4LIVING bible studys

"We all struggle with pressures that hold us back. Becky guides us on a powerful healing journey to flourish in a transformed, grace-filled life. Discover how God takes great pleasure and delight in you. Become free to be your most authentic, beautiful real self!"

—CATHERINE HART WEBER, PhD, Christian therapist, life coach, and spiritual director

"Becky's message is vitally important to all of us followers of Christ. We face a subtle yet powerfully seductive temptation to earn acceptance through performance, and we in the Christian world can fall for it hook, line, and sinker. *Freedom from Performing* pulls the reader into Scriptures and reflections to give a balanced perspective on being set free from the tyranny of performance. How we need Becky's book! I am so grateful for her scripturally based message of grace, and I recommend it highly to churches and individuals as a valuable tool in helping grow disciples."

—NANCIE CARMICHAEL, author of *Surviving One Bad Year* and *Selah*

"Pressure to perform is so ingrained in our culture that we can easily fall into its clutches. Becky Harling reveals the insidious lie that we are somehow defective if we do not perform well and exposes the unconscious root causes that so often fuel our drive to succeed. Writing with incredible insight and compassion, she offers hope. The guided scriptural reflections and exercises at the end of each chapter offer biblically sound, realistic, and practical resources for victoriously growing in freedom."

—HEATHER DAVEDIUK GINGRICH, PhD, associate professor of counseling, Denver Seminary

FREEDOM FROM PERFORMING

GRACE IN AN APPLAUSE-DRIVEN WORLD

BECKY HARLING

NavPress is the publishing ministry of The Navigators, an international Christian organization and leader in personal spiritual development. NavPress is committed to helping people grow spiritually and enjoy lives of meaning and hope through personal and group resources that are biblically rooted, culturally relevant, and highly practical.

For a free catalog go to www.NavPress.com
or call 1.800.366.7788 in the United States or 1.800.839.4769 in Canada.

ISBN-13: 978-1-60006-429-6

Cover design by Arvid Wallen
Cover photo by Michelangelo Gratton, Shutterstock

Some of the anecdotal illustrations in this book are true to life and are included with the permission of the persons involved. All other illustrations are composites of real situations, and any resemblance to people living or dead is coincidental.

Library of Congress Cataloging-in-Publication Data

Harling, Becky, 1957-
Freedom from performing : grace in an applause-driven world / Becky Harling.
p. cm.
Includes bibliographical references.
ISBN 978-1-60006-429-6
1. Grace--Biblical teaching. 2. Grace (Theology)--Textbooks. I. Title.
BT761.3.H38 2011
234--dc22

2011003186

Printed in the United States of America

1 2 3 4 5 6 7 8 / 16 15 14 13 12 11

This book is lovingly dedicated to my wonderful in-laws, Don and Ginny Harling. Thanks, Dad and Mom, for loving me, showing me grace, and being so supportive of the ministry God has given me. And thank you for leaving such a godly legacy for my children and grandchildren.
I love you both!

And to You, Lord Jesus, thanks for Your incredible grace in my life.

CONTENTS

Acknowledgments

Special thanks to:

My husband, Steve—Thanks, babe, for being patient as I finished writing and for supporting me throughout this journey. I love the way you don't color in the lines. Thanks for challenging this rule follower to think outside the box and go for the next challenge. I love you!

My kids: Bethany—You are an amazing and gracious woman and a wonderful mom. I love watching all God is doing through you. Thanks for bringing Tyler into the world. And thank you for letting me process so many ideas from this book with you. I love you, Bethany!

Josiah—Wow! You have become such a remarkable leader. I am so proud of the way God is using you in the lives of so many. Thank you for challenging me to think and grow deeper in my walk with God. I love you, J. J.!

Stefanie—How incredible to watch you become a mother. You have such delightful gifts of perception and insight. I love your passion! Thanks for bringing Charlie into this world. I love you, Stef!

Keri Joy—Your joy is contagious, and your sweet spirit has been such an encouragement to me. I love listening to the songs you write. Never stop singing, Bear; you have such an anointing for leading people into the presence of God. I love you, Bear!

My son-in-law Chris—How I thank God for you! You are such a godly leader and gentle husband to Bethany and an amazing father to Tyler. I love your heart for God and your passion for mercy. I love you, Chris!

My son-in-law Dave—How I thank God for you and your gracious spirit. You consistently have a heart for the broken and bruised. Thank you for the way you love and lead Stef and Charlie. I love you, Dave!

My daughter-in-law Shaina—How I thank God for bringing you into our family! Your gentle, affirming spirit is a rare treasure. I love your heart for those who are hurting. Thank you for the way you always build up J. J. I love you, Shaina!

My precious grandsons, Charlie David and Tyler Josiah—You guys make my Mimi's heart sing. I love you both beyond what you can imagine!

The precious women in Courtney's small group (Courtney Waters, Jill Bartish, Erika Morris, Katherine Elder, Valerie Near) who field-tested this book—Your insights were amazing.

The wonderful women of Foothills Community Church—Thanks for your acceptance and love. I love each of you!

My incredible editor, Liz Heaney—You deserve some type of huge honor! Thank you for your patience as I wrestled through the concepts of this book. There were times I thought I'd never finish, but you cheered me on. Thank you for all the times you let me process. Your wisdom and encouragement are remarkable. I could never do this without you!

The wonderful men and women at NavPress—Thank you for your commitment to seeing life transformation in the lives of God's people. What a privilege to be published by you. Special thanks to Kris Wallen for all your encouragement!

Note to Small-Group Leaders

Small-group leaders are some of the most influential people to assist with life transformation in the kingdom of God. I will be praying for you as you guide the women in your small group during this twelve-week study on internalizing grace. You have the opportunity to be a living model of God's grace to the women in your group.

The Bible study included in this book, "A Daily Dose of Grace," is designed to encourage women in a daily walk with God. Some of the women in your group might not be able to complete every question, and that's okay. Don't discourage them from attending your group even if they have not done the daily study. Offer grace.

Please do everything possible to create a safe, warm, and nonjudgmental environment for your group. I believe with all my heart that God is going to use you in a mighty way as you assist women in internalizing God's grace. Remember, I will be praying for you!

CHAPTER 1

Born to Perform

I am convinced that the basic cause of some of the most disturbing emotional/spiritual problems which trouble evangelical Christians is the failure to receive and live out of God's unconditional grace.

David Seamands

I can still picture the headline: "A Star Is Born." A mixture of shock and excitement coursed through my twelve-year-old body as I realized that our school's sixth-grade newspaper was talking about me. Shy, self-conscious, nerdy, awkward me.

The article, written by a fellow sixth grader, boasted about my performance as Caddie Woodlawn in our class play. For one brief day, tucked into the nightmarish drama of trying to survive middle school, I had the attention and admiration of the smart, cool, popular, and athletic kids. I had found my niche. Lights . . . camera . . . action! Gimme the applause! I was born to perform.

As long as the applause lasted, I felt special. But in the weeks following my rave reviews, I discovered that my life hadn't changed much. I still wore glasses (which I hated) and a lot of hand-me-downs (which were out-of-style). My fans soon forgot all about me.

While that moment in sixth grade stands out in my mind, I have often done things in an effort to get approval and applause, whether from a particular person or a group of people. Sometimes I received the kudos and strokes I craved. Other times I failed miserably, and when the applause didn't come, I felt defeated and very much a loser. I craved an inordinate amount of affirmation from others.

In the religious circles in which I grew up, godliness was defined by how well one followed the rules rather than by gracious life transformation. Instead of being encouraged to bring my sinful nature into the Light, where it could be redeemed and transformed, I felt pressured to push it underneath the surface, where it became fertile soil for secret sins to flourish. I was raised to protect an image rather than become God's image bearer. My identity was rooted in how well I could perform and follow the rules. The fishbowl of public ministry didn't help my struggles any. Instead, it trained me in how to put on a good performance. I learned my role well.

Addicted to approval, I often felt confused or stressed about which commitments to accept and which to reject. I felt like a marionette pulled in a dozen different directions. When I did what was expected of me, I often seethed with resentment. When I said no, I felt overloaded with guilt. I felt a lot of pressure to measure up spiritually but learned little about the role of the Holy Spirit. Instead of learning to rely on His power, I tried harder to be holy. My Christian walk was a well-organized self-improvement course, except I wasn't improving.

I was afraid to let others know the real me, so I hid behind many different masks: the happy mask, the spiritual mask, the pastor's wife mask, the leader mask, and the "I've got everything under control" mask.

On the surface, it seems easier to put on a mask than admit we are fearful, resentful, or—heaven forbid!—sinful. But continually trying to look good keeps us feeling on edge.

Carrying Unnecessary Burdens

Here's the rub: The craving for accolades caused me to become a performance-driven moralist rather than a grace-motivated Christ follower.

The performance-driven woman:

- Becomes a slave to the expectations and demands of others instead of basing her priorities on what she feels the Spirit of God calling her to do
- Compares herself with others, measuring her spirituality and success against others
- Saves face to keep her image intact
- Exhausts herself trying to keep up and feels anxious about whether God is pleased with her
- Pours judgment on others who don't measure up to her standards
- Defines her identity in terms of accomplishment
- Lives for applause from others, becoming disillusioned when the kudos stop

A group of religious leaders in Jesus' day had the same problem. The Pharisees lived for the applause of people. Jesus had this to say about them: "Everything they do is done for men to see: . . . They love the place of honor at banquets and the most important seats in the synagogues" (Matthew 23:5-6). Overly concerned with appearance and prestige, these leaders valued morality, rule following, and putting on a good performance. In their show there was no room for authenticity and life-changing grace. They loved to give rules to others. Jesus confronted them, saying they "tie up heavy loads and put them on men's shoulders" (verse 4).

Many of us grew up in religious systems that tied heavy loads on our backs. As a result, we have developed distorted views of what God desires and whether He feels pleased with us. Author Joanna Weaver describes our warped thinking: "Burdened with the weight of our own spirituality we struggle beneath a load of self-imposed obligations: 'I have to do this . . .' or 'I can't really know God until I do that.'"[1] We carry burdens we were never meant to bear. Consider the following examples:

- Janet agreed to become the classroom mom for her first grader's class, even though she was already overcommitted. Her motivation? She determined long ago to be the best parent possible and felt she had to work hard to achieve her goal. Besides, what would her child's teacher think if she said no?
- Deborah puts on a plastic smile every Sunday morning on her way to church. Even though her heart is breaking over the marriage problems she is facing, she refuses to open up to anyone for fear they would judge her.
- Sarah doesn't talk about her kids much. What would people think if they knew that her children have left their faith?
- Ruth stays late at work every night. The more hours she puts in, the more kudos she receives and the more valuable she feels.
- Sandra takes charge, becoming the director in every social setting. She has advice for everyone. Her mask of being the leader hides her deep insecurities.
- Tara continually whines about her busy schedule, but truth be told, her business makes her feel important.

Do you see yourself mirrored in any of these women? I do! Amazing, the pressure we put on ourselves! Ultimately, we end up believing the lie that if we achieve our own expectations, which are often unrealistic, we will please God more.

I recently attended a party where many of the guests do what I do: write and speak. As I moved around the room, engaging in conversation, many talked with me about their new book contracts, speaking engagements, and radio and TV interviews. All of a sudden I felt myself growing insecure and wanting to talk about myself in order to sound as successful and important as they. Sigh. Driving home from that event, the Spirit of God probed my heart and I heard Him whisper, "Becky, am I pleased with you? Are you significant to Me?"

Ah, good questions. You see, if God is pleased with me, *why* does it matter what others think?

Grace: The Road to Freedom

Jesus introduced a different kind of faith than that of the religious leaders of His day. He offered grace and truth (see John 1:17). He invited the crowds to come to Him authentically: broken, sinful, and weary. He longed for people to find the way of grace. John, one of Jesus' disciples, described it this way: "His commands are not burdensome" (1 John 5:3). Jesus' expectation was that we would receive His grace and that grace would set us free and lighten our load.

You see, our significance doesn't come from what we do or from others and their accolades for our performance. We have intrinsic worth simply because we are made in God's image. It is our true self that God loves, forgives, and longs to surround with grace. Our value is a gift given because of God's grace.

The more we live in God's grace, the more we are freed from the pressure to perform. As author David Seamands wrote, "Grace . . . can make you strong enough and brave enough to take off your superself mask and begin to look at your real self. For it's your real self which God loves and for which Christ died, your real self with all its sins and flaws which He has always known and never stopped loving."[2]

The word *grace* comes from the Greek word *charis*. It speaks of "pleasure, delight, or causes favourable regard."[3] In His grace, God takes great pleasure and delight in us, and He continually offers us His extravagant kindness. God's kindness to us is not measured according to our ability to perform.

GRACE GLIMPSE

Grace means that I am fully known, loved, forgiven, empowered, and pursued by God.

We'll keep coming back to this statement throughout this book because until we live in this truth, we will seek to build our identity and self-worth around other things.

No Room for Pretending

My journey into grace led me to read and reread the parables and other related passages, searching for what was truly important to Jesus. What did I have to do to achieve godliness? Was He calling me to perform better so that I would be acceptable to Him? What was important to Him?

What I love about these parables is that although they preserve truth, they are open-ended. A parable has been described as a "similitude" or "the placing of one thing by the side of another."[4] Parables were simple stories that used common objects or familiar situations to teach hidden truths. Dr. James Boice wrote, "Some sections of the Bible give us grand theology. Some move us to grateful response to God. But the parables break through mere words and make us ask whether there has indeed been any real difference in our lives. . . . No one was ever better than Jesus at getting through pretense to reality."[5] Jesus purposefully left the point of His stories vague so that we would be challenged to think more deeply about their meaning by asking questions. The parables force questions such as *Are you for real*? When we study the parables, we realize there is no room for pretending and performing in Christ's kingdom.

As I studied, I discovered that Jesus didn't make following Him as difficult as many churches make it. He wasn't uptight or stressed out, and the majority of His messages were not hell, fire, and brimstone (except for telling the Pharisees they were "whitewashed tombs"!). What I learned changed me. Jesus was thrilled with me already! In time, with the help of the Holy Spirit, I stopped trying to impress God and started relaxing and simply letting Him love me. Learning to accept God's grace has been the most amazing and freeing experience of my life.

An Invitation

Perhaps your spiritual journey has become drudgery because you too have endeavored to live up to the expectations of others. You've tried so hard, for so long, that you've lost perspective and you're wondering if this thing we call faith is worth all the effort. If so, I invite you to come back to grace. Open your heart and ask the Holy Spirit to help you internalize grace, make it personal, and incorporate it within your sense of self.

In the following pages, I want to share with you what God has been teaching me. In some chapters, we'll study a parable in depth. In others, we'll use it as more of a springboard to other passages. At the end of each chapter, you will find the following three sections:

1. **"Message from the Grace Giver."** These are life-giving truths I drew from Scripture and then recast as if God were speaking them directly to you. I pray they encourage you and help you live in grace.
2. **"Praying Scripture to Internalize Grace."** This section offers help for praying Scripture. I have found that when I pray God's Word back to Him, it helps me take on His grace.
3. **"A Daily Dose of Grace."** This daily Bible study is a great way to spend a bit of time with God each day. It has reflective questions for each day of the week except Sunday. These questions don't have a "right" answer. That might feel challenging if you are a performer, because we performers like to have correct answers. Instead, allow

the questions to help you look inside and figure out your own tendency to perform.

Freedom often comes slowly, so don't get discouraged. Over the last ten years, I have been gradually changing: I am dropping my mask, daring to be authentic, giving up the role of critic, and learning to give myself grace. There is so much more joy in my walk with Christ since I realized He really didn't intend for me to try so hard.

My prayer is that you too will walk away from this study changed—that you will truly understand that you are fully known, loved, forgiven, empowered, and pursued by God. I pray that you will find the courage to peel off your mask, give up the role of performer, and discover the freedom that comes from internalizing God's grace.

Message from the Grace Giver

My child, you have tried so hard for so long to please Me. What you don't realize is that I am already thrilled with you. Don't be like the Pharisees who were always trying to create new rules to please Me. Freedom will come as you find the courage to peel off your mask and receive My grace. You cannot do anything that will cause Me to love you more than I already do. I know you and love you completely, just as you are (see Psalm 139:1-4; 1 John 4:18). As you read this book, come to Me, bring your thoughts to Me, and allow My love to change you.

Praying Scripture to Internalize Grace

Lord, Your Word tells me that it is by grace that I am saved, through faith, and that this faith is a gift from You, not because of anything I have done, so that I can never boast (see Ephesians 2:8-9). Yet I find myself trying so hard to please You. As I go through this study, help me realize that through Christ I have redemption through His blood—the forgiveness of sins in accordance with the riches of God's grace that He lavished on me with all wisdom (see 1:7-8). You accept me completely whether I perform well or not. You invited me to have a relationship with You based completely on Your grace (see Galatians 1:15).

The apostle Paul wrote that it is for freedom that Christ has set us free. He encouraged me to stand firm in my freedom and not be burdened again by the yoke of slavery that comes with the performance lifestyle (see 5:1). Paul also wrote that we shouldn't strive for the approval of others or be obsessed with trying to please them (see 1:10). Lord, You know my tendencies toward stardom and accolades. All around me the world screams that if I am going to be accepted and significant, I need to be successful. In my anguish, I cry out to You. Answer me and set me free (see Psalm 118:5).

When I am tempted to cling to my role as performer, remind me that I am completely known, loved, forgiven, empowered, and pursued by God. Remind me that the Lord my God is with me. He is mighty to save. He takes great delight in me. When I become anxious, He will quiet me with His love and rejoice over me with singing (see Zephaniah 3:17).

A Daily Dose of Grace

Day 1

1. Memorize and meditate on Ephesians 2:8-9 as written here or in another translation:

> It is by grace you have been saved, through faith—and this not from yourselves, it is the gift of God—not by works, so that no one can boast.

2. What does this verse teach about the way to be accepted by God?

3. What part does faith play in our receiving God's grace?

Day 2

1. Read Matthew 23:4-6. How would you describe a Pharisee to someone else? What evidence do we have that the Pharisees lived for the applause of others?

2. Go back and read all of Matthew 23. Seven times in Matthew 23, Jesus begins a sentence with the words "Woe to you" and then goes on to describe or give a word picture of the Pharisees or teachers of the law. List each of the "woe statements" and then write why you think Jesus felt so frustrated with the teachers of the law.

3. Do you think Jesus believed in rules? Please explain.

4. Read Matthew 11:28-30. How did the message of Jesus differ from the message of the other rabbis of His day? What does this verse say to you personally? Write about a time when you felt as though Christ's yoke was neither easy nor light.

Day 3

1. Read Galatians 1:10-17 and 2:9 and then write your own definition of *grace*.

2. Now write the definition given on page 17.
   Grace means . . .

3. Read Galatians 1:10. Do you think the apostle Paul struggled with trying hard to please others? Why, or why not?

Day 4

1. Read Galatians 3:1-3. Do we receive the Holy Spirit by trying harder?

2. Read Galatians 5:1. In what ways are you burdened by "a yoke of slavery"? What would freedom look like in your life?

3. What different masks do you wear? How might those masks hinder your walk with Christ?

4. How can the Holy Spirit help you take off your masks?

Day 5

1. Read 1 John 4:18. What does this verse teach you about how God views you and the kind of relationship He wants to have with you?

2. On a scale of 1 (not important at all) to 10 (very important), how important to you are the opinions of others? How do the expectations of others influence your decisions?

3. How would your life be different if you believed that you are fully known, loved, forgiven, empowered, and pursued by God?

Day 6

1. Review Ephesians 2:8-9.

2. How has your view of God's grace changed this week?

CHAPTER 2

FIND FREEDOM FROM SHAME

Guilt was not my problem as I felt it. What I felt most was a glob of unworthiness that I could not tie down to any concrete sins I was guilty of. What I needed more than pardon was a sense that God accepted me, owned me, held me, and affirmed me, and would never let go of me.

LEWIS SMEDES

I was five years old the first time I heard the song "Amazing Grace." I didn't understand what a wretch was, and when I asked, I was told that a wretch was a very bad person. I remember thinking, *That's me. I'm a wretch. I am dirty and very bad. I must try harder to be good in order for God to like me.*

These thoughts lingered in my mind until I began to understand the correlation between the sexual abuse I experienced as a child and my inability to experience God's grace. My shame about the abuse left me with feelings of guilt, inferiority, self-loathing, and worthlessness. Those feelings, combined with the distorted messages about God that I received from my rigid, rule-oriented upbringing, polluted my understanding of God's grace. I believed that I was not good enough to receive His grace.

I am not alone. While some of us were born more competitive and driven by nature, I believe that many performance issues are rooted in shame. I recently asked a group of women what impact shame has had on their lives. Here are some of the answers I received:

- "As a teenager I was anorexic. I felt so much shame. Fast-forward to becoming an adult. I had a hysterectomy at twenty-six. I wanted children so badly—to be pregnant and give birth. I never did. I felt that I had really screwed up during my anorexic days and that this was my punishment."
- "I remember being abused by my father; I felt tremendous shame. I believed I wasn't worthy of God's grace. Since He let it happen, I was permanently marked as unworthy."
- "When my daughter was one year old, she went through extensive medical testing to determine why she was so small. The reason was genetic, but I felt that God was punishing me because years prior I'd had an abortion. I carried the shame of that abortion for more than twenty-two years, always fearful God would take one of my children to punish me."

Shame drives us to perform, and it prevents us from internalizing God's grace, the very thing that heals our shame. Shame becomes the voice of our accuser, who subtly, yet continually, sends us messages that we are dirty, unclean, deserving of punishment, and beyond being loved by God. Our minds are plagued with doubts such as *Why would God love me? I've messed up so badly. I am such a mess!* In an effort to compensate, we create a persona that we perceive will look better to God and others. We work harder at trying to achieve what we perceive to be God's standards.

Jesus offers another way. The following story is for all of us who have struggled with shame and feelings of ongoing guilt (see Matthew 22:1-14).

THE PARABLE OF THE WEDDING GARMENT

A king prepared a wedding banquet for his son and sent messengers to invite folks to attend. The initial recipients of the invitation declined before receiving the second invitation. This preliminary invitation told guests the date and time of the banquet, similar to our "save the date" announcements. The second invitation, which was formal and official, invited the guests to come at once, as the banquet was ready and the festivities of the marriage celebration were about to begin. Once again, the invitees received the invitation with contempt and indifference. Some of them just ignored it, and others assaulted the king's messengers, even killing them. Enraged, the king sent an army to kill the scoundrels who had murdered his messengers.

Then the king invited the poor and the broken, the good and bad alike, to the banquet. He didn't consider who was worthy to come. It made no difference to him; all were invited. The guests streamed into the banquet hall, ready for the celebration to begin. The king entered and began greeting them. Off in the distance, someone caught his eye. One of the guests was wearing inappropriate clothing. The king approached the man and asked how he got in without the right clothes. The guest had no response, and the king threw him out.

What was going on here? Why did the king toss this guest out? In Jesus' day, it was customary for royalty to send out robes to everyone who would be attending a wedding celebration so that each person would have suitable clothing.[1] The wedding garment was a distinctive, unique robe, so the king could tell immediately that this guest was not dressed properly. If you were to analyze the Greek more closely, you would discover that the guest had deliberately chosen *not* to put on the robe the king had sent for the occasion. This was a flagrant and unthinkable display of disloyalty toward the king, which is why the king had a bouncer throw the guest out of the reception.

In this parable, the wedding garment illustrates God's grace. When we put our faith and trust in Him, He removes our dirty garments of guilt and shame, clothing us instead with Jesus' righteousness.

GRACE GLIMPSE

Grace sets me apart as holy, without spot or blemish. By His grace, God offers to make us completely clean and whole, regardless of our past or how well we perform.

Healthy Shame Versus Unhealthy Shame

If you have received Christ's spotless robe of righteousness, you might be wondering why you still have lingering feelings of guilt and shame. You may wonder why you feel a compulsion to hide from God or put on a mask. The answer lies in the difference between unhealthy shame and healthy shame. Therapist and author Earl Henslin defines healthy shame as "shame that convicts us of sin, prompts us to repent and draws us toward God" and unhealthy shame as "shame that creates spiritual impasse, makes us feel distant from God and causes us to believe we are too bad or somehow unworthy of God's love."[2] Grace provides healing for both healthy and unhealthy shame.

All of us experience a measure of **healthy shame** when we realize that God is completely holy and we are sinful. This realization can prompt us to cry out for God's forgiveness. The prophet Isaiah saw a vision of the Lord in all His holiness. In the vision, angels were circling the throne of God, singing, "Holy, holy, holy is the Lord Almighty; the whole earth is full of his glory" (Isaiah 6:3). Startled, the prophet fell on his face before God and cried, "Woe to me! . . . I am ruined! For I am a man of unclean lips, and I live among a people of unclean lips" (verse 5). The Lord responded in grace, sending one of the angels to Isaiah with this message: "Your guilt is taken away and your sin atoned for" (verse 7).

Healthy shame helps us recognize that although we are created in the image of God, sin has marred that image in us (see Romans 3:23). The good news is that God loves and receives sinners. When we confess to God our sinfulness and ask for His forgiveness, we receive His grace and become His child. We no longer have to pretend we are not sinful. We no longer have to try harder to be good. Just like the king in the story, who offered his guests appropriate clothing to cover their bodies, so God gives us His grace, which covers our shame. From then on, when God looks at us, He sees only the righteousness of Jesus Christ. From that moment on, we never have to feel shame or fear punishment again (see Romans 8:1).

Perhaps you have never told the Lord that you would like to receive His grace. If you would like to do so, here is a sample prayer of what to pray:

> God, I realize I am a person who has sinned. My sin separates me from You and makes me want to hide from You and create a false self that will look better to You. Please forgive me. Thank You, God, that You love me just as I am. You sent Jesus to take the punishment for my sin so that I would no longer have to hide from You. I now place my trust in what Jesus did on the cross for me and receive Your grace. Thank You that I no longer have to fear punishment. From this time on, I belong to You!
>
> Sign and Date ____________________________

If you prayed that prayer with a sincere heart, you have just become a child of God. Romans 10:9 describes the choice you just made: "If you confess with your mouth, 'Jesus is Lord,' and believe in your heart that God raised him from the dead, you will be saved." Never again do you have to fear God's rejection! When you are tempted to doubt this decision, turn back to this page and remind yourself of how you signed and dated your commitment. Then thank God that He heard your prayer. The more you thank Him, the more faith will build in your heart. As God's grace heals our healthy shame, it also heals our unhealthy shame.

Unhealthy shame is the pervasive feeling of not measuring up. It is generally the result of toxic messages we received that make us feel unworthy and dirty, causing us to believe we are not good enough to please others, let alone God. We long for approval, so we work harder and do more. Toxic shame provides the perfect scenario for the creation of a false self. In an effort to look good, we might hide or deny our weaknesses. Or we don masks to make ourselves look better.

Unhealthy shame always prompts hiding. Think about it. When we feel dirty, we hide. This started way back in the Garden of Eden. When Adam and Eve sinned and felt shame, they immediately hid from God and covered their nakedness (see Genesis 3:8-12). Similarly, the shame-driven woman "uses even more energy to cover up and keep secrets by assuming a role—that of the false self. It takes so much energy to keep hiding that there's scarcely energy left for anything else. So often this hiding from yourself and others causes great loneliness and suffering."[3] Hiding keeps us from bringing our shame to the One who can heal those wounds through His grace. Hiding keeps us in bondage to the charade.

God invites us to come out of hiding and stand in His light.

Exposing Unhealthy Shame to the Light of God's Truth

In order to help you do this, I've identified some common sources of shame and then held them up to the light of Scripture. As you read, ask the Holy Spirit to help you see whether you have acscribed to any of these toxic messages and then help you replace them with God's grace and truth.

Constant Criticism: "You Are Not Good Enough"

We internalize the toxic message that we are not good enough when we grow up hearing such things as:

- "What does God think of you when you do *that*?"
- "Why can't you be good, like your sister?"
- "Can't you ever do anything right?"
- "You'll never amount to anything!"
- "How could you be so stupid?"
- "Why don't you ever think?"
- "How can you be so clumsy?"

Such messages don't correct what the person is doing; they criticize that person's being. One author says that the "'you are's' can become a permanent part of our 'I ams.'"[4] Those "I ams" become the voice of a poor self-image: *I am worthless, I am bad, I am ugly, I am stupid*. When we grow up with these critical messages, we feel as though we are deeply flawed. We were created with the need to know we are unconditionally loved and accepted. When we don't receive that in childhood, we can be driven to prove to the world that we are worthy of being accepted.

The Truth: You were created in God's image and as such have intrinsic dignity and self-worth (see Genesis 2:7,22-23). You may have been continually denigrated as a child and even called degrading names, but God calls you precious and holy (see Isaiah 43:4; Colossians 3:12).

Dysfunction or Poverty in Our Family of Origin: "You Should Be Ashamed"

Some people feel driven to perform due to shame and embarrassment they felt about their families while growing up. This was true for my friend Laurie, who had an alcoholic father. No matter what the school event, whether a concert or a graduation, she lived with the fear that her father would show up drunk and embarrass her. Her fears were realized many times. Laurie strove hard to succeed in order to compensate for the embarrassment and shame she felt over her dad's behavior.

Growing up in poverty can also contribute to feelings of shame.

This was the case for two women I know. The shame they felt about never having enough money to purchase clothes has left them with a huge drive to achieve financial success. Although achieving financial success is not necessarily wrong, it can be destructive if it becomes a driving compulsion. Many I know who struggle with this drive to succeed are never satisfied. They never seem to attain the goal of financial stability.

The Truth: You can't take responsibility for the choices of your parents (see Ezekiel 18:20). The amount of money you have has no bearing on how much intrinsic worth you have to God.

Untrue Messages About God: "God Is Not Happy with You"

Some of us feel driven to perform because of wrong messages we received about God—that He is a demanding taskmaster, angry and disappointed when we don't perform well enough. This was the case for Bonnie. She told me,

> My prayer life suffers from my religious upbringing. I heard many times "Your prayers will hit the ceiling if there is unconfessed sin in your life. God doesn't hear." How many hours I have spent wanting and needing to go to God in prayer, but instead I list out all the sins I can think of and then fall asleep or run out of time. I never get to praise or petition.

The Truth: God loves to listen to your prayers. Praying is simply conversing with Him. He doesn't keep a checklist of sins confessed versus sins unconfessed before He hears your prayers (see Matthew 6:5; Romans 8:26). I have found that I am often not aware of sinful attitudes I have until I am deeply engaged in worship. So often, it is there on my knees, as I am worshipping, that the Holy Spirit will bring conviction about sin.

Childhood Abuse: "I Must Be Bad"

Performers who experienced abuse in childhood—whether sexual, emotional, or physical—often see themselves as responsible for the abuse. They absorb the shame of the abuser, thereby concluding, *The abuse is bad; therefore, I must be bad. I must try harder to be good.* Those thought patterns linger, even into adulthood.

This was certainly true in my life. As I mentioned earlier, I was sexually abused as a little girl. That abuse left scars of shame in my life. As an adult, I felt obsessed with holiness. I longed for God to make me pure and holy, even perfect. When I sinned, I confessed but then obsessed over my wrongdoing and ultimately spiraled into self-loathing and despair. Why couldn't I be the godly woman I wanted to be? Why couldn't I master the fruit of the Spirit? I didn't realize how many of my thoughts were emotionally and spiritually unhealthy until I began to receive counseling to help me find healing for the abuse.

The Truth: Abuse is always the abuser's fault, never the victim's. The shame belongs to those who harmed you, not to you. You cannot orchestrate atonement for another person's sin (see Psalm 49:7-8). You can only offer them forgiveness.

Personal Failure: "I Can't Forgive Myself for What I Did"

When we strive for perfection, personal failure can feel devastating and heap on the shame, causing us to try harder to meet our own expectations. One author wrote, "Shame occurs when a failure in our performance or a flaw in our appearance is considered so important that it solidifies a negative self-concept."[5]

One night Tammy confessed to me that she had engaged in an extramarital affair many years before. Her "dirty little secret" had haunted her for years. She begged God to forgive her, but she continued to live in a prison to shame. She's petrified that if people find out what she did they will think less of her. Tammy wants others to perceive her as a godly leader. Her failure has led her to try harder as a Sunday school teacher. It's almost as if she is working to achieve atonement for her sin. She never lets others get too close emotionally. She lives in isolation, striving harder and harder to make up for her moral failure, fearful that someone will discover the very thing she is hiding.

The Truth: You cannot make atonement for your sins. God forgives your sins and cleanses you completely (see 1 John 1:9). You need to receive His grace so that you can wear your new robe with confidence (see Hebrews 2:17; Romans 3:25).

God's grace continually heals your shame as you stand firm in His righteous robe that declares you holy and dearly loved. Only as you stand confidently in that robe are you able to find freedom from performing.

Wear Your Righteous Robe with Confidence

Isaiah 61:3 provides us the wisdom we need to stand in our clean robe and leave the dirty clothing of shame far behind. Isaiah wrote, "Bestow on them a crown of beauty instead of ashes, the oil of gladness instead of mourning, and a garment of praise instead of a spirit of despair." I see in this verse three distinct gifts Christ gives us when we become His daughters, so that we can stand confidently, free from shame: a crown of beauty, the oil of gladness, and garments of praise.

1. A crown of beauty. In its original meaning, the crown of beauty was an "ornamental headdress like a crown or a wedding veil."[6] This was a headdress a woman wore on her wedding day to identify her as the bride. The crown portrayed strength and dignity and set the bride apart.

In biblical times, ashes symbolized mourning. When Tamar, King David's daughter, was raped by her half brother Amnon, she "put ashes on her head and tore the ornamented robe she was wearing. She put her hand on her head and went away, weeping aloud as she went" (2 Samuel 13:19). Because of her half brother's sexual assault, she was clothed in shame.

Some of you know the devastation and degrading aftermath of rape. God's heart is with you. He understands. He invites you to mourn the dignity and innocence stolen from you. He longs to comfort you. In His grace, He offers you a crown of beauty to replace your ashes.

Others of you experienced the ashes of other kinds of shame: shameful messages from your childhood, feelings of shame because of personal moral failure, and so on. The Grace Giver lovingly brushes the ashes off your head, and in their place He puts the crown of beauty. He wants you to wear that crown of beauty with your head held high. The ashes of past shame are gone.

Whenever I am tempted to go back to the laundry basket filled with dirty clothes of shame, I stop and visualize myself wearing my righteous robe with a crown of beauty on my head. I have a bracelet that helps me do this. For one of my birthdays, a close friend gave me a bracelet with three charms. One charm is a heart, to remind me that I am deeply loved. Another is a butterfly, to remind me that I have become a new creation in Christ Jesus. The last charm is a crown, to remind me that my beloved Jesus has removed the ashes of my shame and replaced them with a crown of beauty. Every now and then, when shame threatens to capture my thoughts, I put on my bracelet and remind myself that I am wearing a crown of beauty. This helps me stand confidently in strength and dignity.

2. The oil of gladness. The second gift is the Holy Spirit. In the Bible, oil was used for medicinal purposes, healing, anointing a person to a position of authority, and consecration. In the New Testament, it was also a symbol of the Holy Spirit.[7] When we receive God's saving grace and put on His robe of righteousness, we receive the Holy Spirit. He lives within us, continually healing our shame and replacing our mourning with gladness. The Holy Spirit not only indwells us but also anoints us and gives us authority over the evil one, who tries continually to rob us of our gladness. The Holy Spirit consecrates us, continually transforming us into the image of Jesus Christ.

In my journey to freedom from performing, I learned that try as I might, I could not let go of my shame. I had to lean into the Holy Spirit, moment by moment. When shameful thoughts hammered my mind and I felt strong urges to up my performance, I whispered a prayer to the Holy Spirit, asking Him to heal whatever wound was being triggered and remind me that I am deeply loved and cherished. I asked Him to heal me of the driving compulsion to perform better. As I have consistently asked the Holy Spirit to heal my shame, He has answered. Gradually, I am finding new freedom!

3. Garments of praise. It is a gift to be able to praise the Lord. The more we choose to praise God for His love, forgiveness, and the dignity He offers us, the more the Holy Spirit quickens our hearts to believe we are loved just as we are. The more we praise God for clothing us in His righteousness, the more our hearts believe we are clothed in righteousness. The less we find ourselves controlled by shame, the more joy we experience. God's Word says that "instead of their shame my people will receive a double portion . . . and everlasting joy will be theirs" (Isaiah 61:7).

I have seen the truth of this Scripture in my own life. Satan would love nothing better than to have me sink into a pit of despair. But this I know: Satan cannot stand when I am praising God. He is conquered by my praise. One author put it this way: "Satan is allergic to praise, so when there is massive triumphant praise, Satan is paralyzed, bound and banished."[8] So when shameful thoughts fill me with despair, I praise God that He loves me and declares me holy. I praise Him that there is no condemnation or punishment for me, even when I fail (see Romans 8:1). I praise Him that He sees me as holy, and joy fills my heart.

God's grace continually heals our shame as we stand firm in His righteous robe that declares us holy and dearly loved. My question for you is this: Will you receive and put on the garment of praise, or will you go back to the clothes of despair? If you are like me, you will be tempted to run back to the laundry basket, pull out the dirty clothes of shame, and put them on once again. Let me show you what I mean.

As a parent, I have longed to do it "right," whatever *right* means. I often second-guess myself as a parent. Recently, one of my adult daughters confronted me because she felt I was nagging her and not allowing her the freedom to fail. I apologized, and then my mind immediately filled with such thoughts as, *You're never going to be healed of your controlling spirit. You are going to ruin your relationship with your adult daughter. You grew up in an unhealthy situation and now you are passing that on to your kids*. But then the Spirit of God interrupted my thoughts and reminded me, "Becky, you have left those old clothes behind. Don't dig them out and put them back on. Stand in My healing. You've apologized. Now praise Me for how I am changing you. Praise Me that you stand complete in My righteousness!"

Dear performer, God wants to heal your shame. You do not have to hide your sins or the sins committed against you. Bring them to the feet of the Grace Giver. He will not condemn you (see Romans 8:1). He will forgive you (see 1 John 1:9) and heal you. He invites you to come out of hiding and stand in the light of His grace, where you are fully known. He invites you to take off the dirty clothes of shame and receive the clean robe of His righteousness.

Message from the Grace Giver

> My child, your thinking has been warped by so many toxic messages. Come to Me and allow Me to heal your shame. Lay aside those messages and allow Me to fill your mind with truth (see Romans 12:2). Wear My righteous robe with strength and dignity. I paid a high price for your robe because I love you! I long to heal the wounds that trigger shame in your soul. Sink into My grace. Allow Me to crown you with dignity. Permit My Spirit to erase those old messages and replace them with My truth. Leave the shameful clothes of despair behind and

put on the garments of praise. As you do this, you will find joy and freedom!

Praying Scripture to Internalize Grace

I delight greatly in You, God; my soul rejoices in You, for You have clothed me with the garments of salvation and arrayed me in a robe of righteousness (see Isaiah 61:10). I praise You for my righteous robe. I praise You that Your righteousness is a complete gift. There is nothing I can do to earn righteousness.

When I placed my faith and trust in the atoning work of Jesus Christ on the cross, You clothed me in Your righteousness (see 2 Corinthians 5:21). You said that if I confess with my mouth that Jesus is Lord and believe in my heart that You raised Him from the dead, I will be saved (see Romans 10:9). How I praise You that You didn't make it more complicated than that. You have promised that anyone who trusts in You will never be put to shame (see Romans 10:11). Thank You that I now wear Your righteousness robe (see Romans 3:21). I don't have to worry about being good enough to wear it! I only have to receive it. It's incredible to me that now when You look at me, I look as good to You as Your Son, Jesus Christ! I praise You, God!

You have promised that those who look to You will be radiant and that their faces will never be covered with shame (see Psalm 34:5). You have promised that no one whose hope is in You will ever be put to shame (see Psalm 25:3). Teach me to relax in the luxury of my new robe and not head back to the dirty clothing of shame. Show me how to feel at ease in Your righteous robe. Help me to wear it with strength and dignity (see Proverbs 31:25).

Holy Spirit, You are the guarantor of God's grace. You are the seal of ownership for the righteous robe I wear (see 2 Corinthians 1:22). You have the power to transform my life (see 2 Corinthians 3:17-18). I need Your help in holding my shame up to the light of Your truth. I cannot internalize grace on my own. Thank You that You guide me into all truth (see John 14:17). Teach me to live in complete dependence on You.

A DAILY DOSE OF GRACE

Day 1

1. Memorize and meditate on 1 Corinthians 6:11 as written here or in another translation:

   > You were washed, you were sanctified, you were justified in the name of the Lord Jesus Christ and by the Spirit of our God.

2. What were some of the toxic messages you received growing up that produced shame in your life? List them here.

3. Describe the difference between healthy shame and unhealthy shame.

4. Read Romans 10:9-13. What does this passage teach about how God's grace can heal both our healthy shame and our unhealthy shame?

Day 2

1. Read Matthew 22:1-14, and then answer the following questions.
   a. What was the response to the first invitation?

   b. What was the response to the second invitation?

   c. How did the third invitation differ from the first two?

   d. What does this parable teach us about grace?

Day 3

1. Read Romans 3:21-26. According to this passage, what is the source of our righteousness?

2. Who is the only One qualified to atone for our sins?

3. How did He do this?

4. How is the atonement of Christ indicative of God's justice? How do grace and justice meet at the cross?

Day 4

1. Read Romans 8:1. If you have become a child of God by receiving His grace, you do not have to fear punishment by God, even if you do something wrong. How does this verse heal your need to create a false self?

2. Read 2 Corinthians 5:21. According to this verse, what did Christ do that we might receive healing from both healthy shame and unhealthy shame? Now how does God see us?

3. Read 2 Corinthians 5:17. What happens after you receive God's grace and become His child?

4. Read 1 John 4:17. According to this verse, why are we able to have confidence and not fear punishment from God?

Day 5

1. Read Isaiah 61:1-3 and then answer the following questions. (Isaiah is speaking prophetically here about the ministry of Jesus Christ.)
   a. How does Christ bring beauty out of our ashes?

   b. How does He give the oil of gladness instead of mourning?

   c. How does He give garments of praise instead of despair?

   d. How can you wear the crown of beauty with strength and dignity?

2. Write a prayer of praise based on Isaiah 61:1-3. Thank God for each gift (the crown, the oil of the Holy Spirit, and praise). He offers to help in the healing of your shame.

Day 6

1. Review 1 Corinthians 6:11.

2. Read Ephesians 3:12. Because of God's grace, how are we to approach His throne?

3. How are freedom and confidence related?

4. What would it look like in your life to approach the throne of God with freedom and confidence?

BUILD A ROCK-SOLID CORE

When we live a life centered around what others like, feel, and say, we lose touch with our own identity.

NEVA COYLE

"Becky, you are living as though every appointment is an audition!"

My friend's words stunned me and prompted some deep introspection. As I thought back over recent appointments, I realized there was an element of truth in what she said. In my quest for personal growth, I analyzed my performance after every appointment. Whether I'd met with someone for lunch, with someone looking to share her heart, or with someone I was mentoring or encouraging, I evaluated how the appointment went: *How did I come across? Did I ask enough questions? Did I listen well? Was my communication clear?*

I did the same thing anytime I spoke somewhere. The moment I sat down, my internal evaluations began: *Did I tell enough engaging stories? Did I use enough Scripture? Did I rely on my notes, or did I depend on the Holy Spirit? How responsive was the audience? Did people laugh at my jokes? Did they seem interested and engaged? How did they respond after the message? How many approached me for prayer?*

As I thought about what my friend had observed in me, I realized that my core identity was built on other people's opinions of me. I had created a false self. The false self is "an identity rooted in secondary things like accomplishments, productivity, people pleasing, fame, or success. The false self is always an identity that can be lost because it is a self we develop."[1]

A Shaky Identity

When God originally created men and women, Adam and Eve, He formed them in His image. Their identities were rooted solely in being deeply loved by the One who created them. They enjoyed unbroken fellowship with Him in the garden. They were naked (nothing was hidden) and "felt no shame" (Genesis 2:25). You remember the rest of the story. Satan came to the garden and tempted Eve, and she broke God's command to not eat the forbidden fruit and convinced Adam to follow suit. In a moment of disobedience, sin entered the world (see Genesis 3:1-10).

Since that time, everyone is born with a broken identity. As we saw in the last chapter, we put on masks, hoping to cover our shame. We hide our true self, hoping our mask will help us feel more loved, more significant, more worthwhile. We run after applause, affirmation, and accolades in order to validate our self-worth. Without even realizing it, we create an illusionary self with the hope of gaining affirmation and work hard all our lives to excel in something, such as music, entertainment, teaching, or academics. That expertise leads to affirmation, which prompts us to want to show only "the expert" to the world around us. That's why we often feel compelled to tell people what we do when we meet them.

We have built our identity around the following equation found in Robert S. McGee's profound book *The Search for Significance*:

Self-Worth = Performance + Others' Opinions[2]

This equation is a lie from Satan. If he can keep us believing that this equation is correct, he knows we will not experience God's grace. Many women are living this equation right now, continually wondering, *What's wrong with me? Why can't I get it right?* or *Why am I so insecure?* If you are asking these questions, it's a sign that your identity is built on shaky ground.

Dear reader, there is another way. Jesus once told a woman that those who worship Him must do so in spirit and truth (see John 4). If we are going to worship God in truth, we must let go of our idols (success, status, applause, accomplishment) and the false self we've created in order to get those things. Jesus invites us back to our true selves, in all our brokenness, and encourages us to build our core identity on His grace alone. Only then will we find the freedom to stop performing.

Let's take a look at a story Jesus told that illustrates this point (see Luke 6:46-49).

THE PARABLE OF THE TWO BUILDERS

One day as the crowds gathered around Him, Jesus told a story about two builders. One builder was wise, the other foolish. The wise builder visited several properties and settled near the mountains. He dug his foundation down deep into the rock, giving his house a rock-solid core.

The foolish builder, however, wanted beachfront property. (Who could blame him? I love the beach!) On the surface, his home looked lovely, but there was a big problem: He hadn't taken the time to dig a foundation. Jesus doesn't tell us why. Perhaps the builder didn't seek wise counsel, or maybe he simply didn't want to put the time and effort into something so boring. Whatever the reason, he built his home without a foundation.

At this point in the story, Jesus has the attention of every listener. I can just imagine a few builders in the crowd chuckling and shaking their heads, thinking, *What an idiot! Who would build a house without a foundation?* They knew what would happen next. The waterfront home would not be able to withstand the storms that hit Palestine during rainy season. During most of the year, Palestine enjoyed lovely weather, but "during the rainy season heavy rains with excessive flooding could wash away poorly grounded homes.[3] The crowd knows that a home on the beach without a foundation would be destroyed.

As the chuckling dies down, Jesus throws in the teaching point: "The one who hears my words and does not put them into practice is like a man who built a house on the ground without a foundation. The moment the torrent struck that house, it collapsed and its destruction was complete" (verse 49). Those listening that day had to be asking themselves, *What words is Jesus talking about?*

I believe He was talking about His message of grace.

Christ's Life Message

If I were to summarize the essence of Christ's life message, I would say it was grace. Jesus came as living proof of God's grace. When we accept grace, it infuses the core of who we are. Every part of our identity flows out of the fact that we are completely known, loved, forgiven, empowered, and pursued by God. We don't need the false self anymore. Our gifts, abilities, and personality flow out of the foundational truth that we are *already* loved and cherished. We don't feel the need to earn God's approval; we already have it. When the storms come (and by storms I mean failure, disappointment, or rejection), our core identity will stand unshaken. But if we don't build our identity on the foundation of God's grace, we will crash.

Think about it. Let's say you build your identity around your career. What happens if you lose your job? All of a sudden you wonder, *Who am I?* Or suppose you build your identity around your marriage and the unthinkable happens: Your husband walks out on you. On top of being brokenhearted and lonely, you struggle with feelings of meaninglessness and emptiness. You wonder if life is worth living. Or let's say your identity is built around your looks. Time marches on and one day you look in the mirror at wrinkles and gray hair and wonder, *Where is the young woman who once was so alive?* We cannot risk building our identity on anything less than God's grace. This is the grace principle found in the parable of the wise and foolish builders.

GRACE GLIMPSE

God's grace is the only sure foundation for my identity.

The Impact of a Grace-Filled Core

When you build your core identity on God's grace, you are set free in every area of your life. Let me show you what I mean.

Imagine a wheel with eight spokes connected to a circle in the center. The wheel represents your life, and the spokes represent different aspects of your life. The circle in the center represents Christ's grace. Each of these eight aspects brings with it expectations, whether yours or others'. Let's look at each of these and see how living out of a grace-filled core can affect that part of your life.

1. Spiritual

This is your relationship with God. If you are trying to earn God's acceptance or atone for your sin, you will be spinning your wheels. As hard as you try, you cannot be perfect, and because God is perfect, you will continually feel inadequate and that you can't please Him.

God's only requirement for forgiveness of sins is that we receive His grace. When we do, we don't have to fear God's rejection or His punishment. We can rest in His forever forgiveness, knowing that Jesus took our punishment. He came to die and take the punishment for every sin we would ever commit. His sacrifice on the cross was complete. It satisfied God's anger toward our sin and wiped away our need to be punished (see Hebrews 10:8-14). As a result, we never have to fear His punishment again; His work is complete.

I have met many women who think God is punishing them whenever life is not going well. This seems particularly true for women who have had an abortion and then struggle to get pregnant. Oh, dear reader, God does not punish you when you sin or mess up! That is a lie from Satan. Jesus has paid the price for sin in full! It is finished. If you have received His grace, He promises that "there is now no condemnation for those who are in Christ Jesus" (Romans 8:1). Although sin sometimes has consequences, let's not confuse consequences with punishment.

When God looks at you, you look as good to Him as Jesus does (see 2 Corinthians 5:21). Wow, take a moment and think about that. Grace tells you that God will never reject you; He has set His pleasure on you. He loves you completely and categorically. Others may not deem you worthy of love, but God loves you unconditionally. Others may not pursue you, but God continually and passionately pursues you. You don't have to fear rejection from Him, because His acceptance of you is not based on your performance; it's based on His grace.

Rather than striving to perform for God, why not just respond to His love? Every morning, before you get out of bed, pray,

> *Lord, I thank You that I am fully known, loved, forgiven, and empowered by You. I don't have to live in fear today that I will not live up to Your expectations. I receive all Your grace today, and I just want to love You in return. At some points today, I am going to fail, but Lord Jesus, how I praise You that Your feelings for me won't change. Show me how to live in Your grace today.*

That's what it means to live out of a grace-filled core.

2. *Familial*

Family is so important to each of us, yet family expectations can be the most difficult to handle. We love our families so much, but we can not possibly meet all their needs. If we try to do this, we will end up exhausted and burned out.

I polled fifty women and asked them where they felt the most pressure to perform. The leading answer was motherhood. If ever there was a guilt-producing role, it is that of being a mom. A friend who is a therapist has a pillow in her office that reads, "If it's not one thing, it's your mother."

It's easy for moms to live in constant fear that their children will need to spend thousands of dollars in therapy because of their upbringing. However, parenting out of a grace-filled core means realizing we are not going to parent perfectly, accepting that we are going to make mistakes and that sometimes those mistakes will be big. However, if we parent from a grace-filled identity, when we mess up we have the courage to apologize because we are secure in the grace Christ offers. We don't have to save face with our kids, pretending to have it all together. When our identity is imbued with Christ's grace, we have the courage to apologize and say that we were wrong. When we fail, we say to God, *Thank You for this opportunity to experience Your grace once again.* When our children watch us fail and receive God's grace, they gain an understanding of how grace works. It draws them to Christ; it doesn't repel them from Him.

The second area where the women I polled said they felt the most pressure to perform was in their marriages. Many felt they were not measuring up to their husband's expectations and had given up. When we live out of a grace-filled core, we can minister to our husband's needs because we love him rather than because we are trying to find our significance in being loved by him. Instead, we find our significance in God's love and are able to love our husbands out of the overflow of a full heart. This is what Diane learned.

She and her husband brought a performance mentality into their marriage. He demanded perfection from her, and many nights she fell into bed sobbing, wondering if she could stay in a marriage where she felt she could never do enough. One day as she was reading about grace in the book of Romans, the light went on in her head. Diane fell to her knees and cried, *Lord, I have replaced one religious system with another. I confess that I am continually trying to measure up. Please, God, allow me to receive Your grace to the core of who I am. I want to begin to experience Your love. I want the assurance that nothing can separate me from Your love.*

When I asked Diane how that prayer changed her marriage, she said,

> It didn't. It changed me. When my husband's demands became unreasonable (and they often did), I began to realize that my significance was found in God's love, and that gave me the freedom to lovingly say no. Internalizing God's gracious love gave me the security I needed to set boundaries. Slowly, I began to realize that even when I couldn't feel my husband's love, I could nestle down in the love that Christ offered. Ultimately, that truth set me free.

We often think of the ripple effect of sin as being huge. And it is. But the ripple effect of grace is even bigger. When we function within our family systems out of a grace-filled identity, the ripple effect is huge. I have watched God redeem family situations that were horrific, all because one person chose to receive God's grace.

3. Vocational

Every vocation has expectations and pressures to perform. If you don't do a good job, it's likely you will get fired. And God values a good work ethic. But you can have a strong work ethic and still not build your identity around what you do. How? By reminding yourself every day that your work does not define you.

No matter how successful or unsuccessful you are vocationally, God's feelings about you don't change. When who you are is deeply rooted in His grace, you give yourself permission to continue to grow and to accept that you are not going to get it all perfect. And you trust that the Holy Spirit will empower you to do whatever God has called you to do.

Jesus promised to leave His Spirit to dwell inside us (see John 14:16-17). When He ascended back into heaven, after His death and resurrection, He said, "You will receive power when the Holy Spirit comes on you" (Acts 1:8). When we become followers of Jesus Christ, His Spirit takes up residency in our bodies. From then on, we have the indwelling Christ living within us, continually empowering us. So anytime you feel inadequate or fear failure, remember that the Holy Spirit is there, willing and able to help. He even promises that His power is more clearly seen in our weaknesses (see 2 Corinthians 12:9).

I learned this the hard way. The first time I sent a book proposal to a publisher, it was rejected. I felt devastated and went for a long walk and a good cry. I had been so excited and *positive* that God was calling me to write. What had gone wrong? After praying about it, I decided to try again. I ended up revising that proposal for two more submittals, but still it was rejected. I'd failed not once but three times! My mind reeled with self-doubt: "I can't write. I wish I were smarter. God, why didn't you design me with a better brain?" And finally, I decided to quit. "I'll never be able to write!"

My husband told me he felt that God wasn't going to give me a book contract until my identity didn't depend on me being a writer. I remember wishing Steve would keep his thoughts to himself! My mentor chimed in, reminding me that God was doing a deep work in me. Her exact words were, "God is still shaping the message you are called to write." She didn't feel as though it were the right time to quit, and she reminded me that God would empower me as I continued. She encouraged me to try again, this time with a writing coach to help me get started. I felt skeptical and more than a little discouraged but decided to pray about it.

The next day, I went to the beach by myself. I walked, I cried, and I prayed. I questioned God about whether writing was truly my calling. If it were, then why was I continually failing? Finally, I sat down, shut up, and listened for His voice. While I was sitting on the beach, the Holy Spirit reminded me that my identity could not be tied up in whether or not I got published. (It bugs me when the Holy Spirit's voice sounds strangely like my husband's!) He whispered that I was His beloved child, I hadn't failed, and I didn't have to impress Him or anyone else with my writing ability. Sigh. Then He gave me an idea for how to restructure the book I was trying to write. I decided to give it another shot, and the end result was a book contract.

God often calls us to big challenges that feel impossible. His desire is not that we back away thinking, *If I can't do this perfectly, I don't want to try* or *If I don't get this right the first time, I'll never get it right and should give up.* Instead, He invites us to lean into His grace for strength, resting in the truth that He will help us do what He calls us to do. I have found that God often calls me to tasks that are beyond my natural abilities. He desires that I understand that He is the One who will do it through me! That is one of the functions of His Spirit.

4. Intellectual

A few years ago, a friend of mine whose husband is extremely bright pulled out a Mensa credit card. I was fascinated. I thought for sure the Mensa credit card was for women in menopause. (The Mensa society is a nonprofit organization for those who have scored at least 98 percent on standardized IQ tests.) Obviously, I don't have one of those credit cards, and there have been times in my life when I wished I were smarter than I am.

When Christ's grace is at the core of who we are, we accept the intelligence we've been given and stop beating ourselves up for not being smarter. We know that in God's economy, wisdom is more valued than intelligence. The Bible never talks about the mind in terms of the amount of *intelligence* a person possesses; it speaks in terms of the *wisdom* a person possesses. Wisdom, reflected in the choices we make, comes as we allow the Holy Spirit to govern our minds. This is why the apostle Paul wrote that "the mind controlled by the Spirit is life and peace" (Romans 8:6). Our minds are powerful tools as far as setting the stage for our emotions.

5. Emotional

We were created to experience a wide range of emotions: joy, happiness, hope, sadness, anger, and frustration, to name a few. It's good and right to feel these emotions. Many of us, however, feel frightened when we experience negative emotions, so we run, hide, or go to the opposite extreme and pitch our tent in the campground of negativity and sink into despair.

When we grow in our understanding of grace, we are free to experience negative emotions without feeling overwhelmed by them. We feel pain but rest in the comfort that our feelings don't change who we are. Our feelings may go up and down, but when our core identity is built on the rock-solid foundation of Christ's grace, it stands secure. We know that nothing can change the fact that He loves us completely and that He is well pleased with us (see Luke 3:22).

6. Physical

Most women place a high priority on beauty. This is right and good because God created us to reflect His beauty. But often we draw our significance from how well we think we meet our culture's standard of beauty. If we feel beautiful, we feel significant. But our self-worth plummets if we are having a bad body day. (You know what I mean — those days when you'd just rather not have any mirrors in your house!)

A part of God's grace is that He leaves His Spirit to dwell in us. That changes dramatically how we view our physical bodies, because they are the sanctuary of the living God. We are significant because our bodies are beautiful cathedrals where the presence of Christ dwells.

I distinctly remember the Sunday before I was diagnosed with breast cancer. I'd had the biopsy the previous Monday and was waiting for the results. That morning in church, we sang, "Lord, Prepare Me to Be a Sanctuary." The Holy Spirit spoke softly from within my soul, asking, "Becky, will you let me use your body to glorify Myself?" I knew in that moment that the biopsy results would be positive. Looking back, I can see that God glorified Himself through the physical pain I suffered as well as through the changes my body encountered. The double mastectomy I experienced has opened more doors than I can count to share the living Christ with others.

7. Social

We were created for community, and relationships are integral to every part of our lives. However, expectations in those relationships can cause problems. Many women are people pleasers at heart and try to keep up with the expectations of friends or coworkers. They don't want to disappoint them. Other women have expectations of others. Either tendency causes problems. If we try to please others and meet their expectations for us, we will lose our sense of self and may burn out from exhaustion. If we set expectations for others, we will feel disappointment and anger when they fail.

In contrast, if we have a grace-filled core, we'll implement boundaries when others want us to meet their expectations, and we'll love our friends out of the overflow of a full heart and offer them grace.

8. Missional

What do I mean by missional? I am referring to the aspect of our lives where we intentionally join God in His mission to demonstrate grace and love to the world.

Once Christ's grace is solidly at our core, we are able to serve others in our neighborhoods, our communities, and the world. We don't serve because we are trying to be good or to make God happy; we serve because our lives have been so transformed by Christ's grace that we are excited to reflect that grace to the world in which we live. We begin to pray, *Lord, live Your life through me. Let others experience Your grace as I have.* We are going to come back to this point in chapter 5 when we talk about finding one's purpose and passion.

Rebuilding

To rebuild your identity on the foundation of grace:

Dig up the old foundation. When there are significant cracks in the foundation of a house, you have to dig up the old foundation before you lay a new one. This was certainly the case for me. I had to take a look at some of the core beliefs I had accumulated in childhood. I asked myself questions like these: *What exactly do I believe about God? Do I believe He is angry and emotionally distant? Do I believe He is a demanding taskmaster? What do I believe to be true about myself? Do I believe I am loveable?* I asked the Holy Spirit to guide me as I analyzed the messages I had received about God. I also talked with a counselor and godly mentor as I processed my thoughts.

I came to see that the reason I felt so driven to perform for God was that my identity was built on the foundational belief that God will be pleased with me if I work hard for Him and prove myself to Him. As I looked back, I could see how I had arrived at this belief. My childhood was very rule oriented: no dancing, no cards, and no movies. I heard a lot about serving God, which I took to mean, "God likes you better if you follow the rules and serve Him." I had to dig up that foundation before I could lay a new one.

Develop a new schema. Our schema is the conceptual framework around which we build our life. I began developing a new schema for my life that was based on my definition of grace: "I am fully known, loved, forgiven, and empowered by God. Nothing I do can either add or subtract from that truth." My new schema encouraged me to change my self-talk. Often the messages I told myself were not positive, let alone true.

What about you? Stop and think for a moment. How many times a day do you try to meet someone's expectations so that you will feel their approval? How many times a day do you think, *I can't do this*? If you realize that your thoughts often turn in this direction, you need a new schema—one that God can use so the truth of grace will penetrate your soul. Think about taking a minute to memorize the definition of grace mentioned in the previous paragraph. Write it on an index card and tape it to your mirror. Every morning as you are putting on your makeup, repeat the definition and meditate on it. It will become your new self-talk. The more you rehearse this new schema, the more the truth of grace will penetrate your soul.

Drop your "shoulds." I had a lot of "shoulds," and most of them revolved around imaginary expectations. I went through life thinking such things as *I should read my Bible more* (even though I read my Bible every day), *I should pray more* (even though I prayed every day), *I should entertain more* (even though for most of our ministry life we've had people in our home continually), *I should read to my children more* (even though I read to them every night). My list of shoulds governed my life and produced a lot of guilt. Ultimately, my shoulds kept me from experiencing God's grace.

How many times a day do you say, "I should"? That phrase only produces guilt, and guilt is not from God. Instead, try this. Next time you start saying, "I should," say, "I want." For example, instead of saying, "I should love God more," try, "I want to love God more." Or instead of saying, "I should read my child a story," how about, "I would like to read my child a story. I can't today, but I will tomorrow."

Define your priorities. This helped me a lot. For example, when I realized that one of my priorities was spending time with my husband and children, I didn't struggle as much with guilt if I turned down invitations in order to have more time with my family. When I realized that another of my priorities was teaching God's Word, I didn't feel guilty if I said no to other Christian service opportunities so that I could focus on improving my communication skills.

Ask God to showcase His grace through you. God is weaving His story of redemption throughout all of history. Each of our stories is one tiny piece of a far greater story. When we realize that we are a small part of what God is doing in history, it helps us interpret the events of our lives differently. Rather than interpreting trials and sorrow as punishment from God, we begin to see that God can use the sorrow and suffering He allows in our lives to showcase His grace. When we realize that God is using our story, we give up being the star of our own show.

When I did this, I no longer felt embarrassed and ashamed about my story. I began to focus on the fact that God had brought me healing and was using my pain and what I had learned to help other women. He used the sorrow and suffering of cancer, childhood sexual abuse, and other difficult things in my life to birth a life message that He can bring beauty out of brokenness. He redeemed my story, and it became a showcase of His grace.

What Message Does Your Life Speak?

The storms of life are going to come. Each of us will experience failure, sorrow, pain, and disappointment. These difficulties, though trying, provide the material for the message our lives will send to others. Some people's lives speak a message of hope; other people's lives speak a message of despair. What message does your life speak? If you build your core identity around God's grace, your life will have meaning and purpose because your story will be a showcase for God's grace. Author Nancie Carmichael wrote, "When you allow God's grace fully into your disappointments and failures, He will give you an honest and strong message that you can share with others."[4]

As we conclude this chapter, get alone with God and ask Him to search your heart. Ask Him to unmask your false self and show you what you have built your core identity on. Then ask Him for wisdom as you begin to rebuild. Maybe spend some time writing out your life story, and as you record different events, ask God for the wisdom to show you what your core has been built on. Perhaps it's time to do a little archaeological dig and lay a new foundation.

Message from the Grace Giver

> Dear performer, you are living your life in bondage to so many people. Though you desire their approval, you will not be able to measure up to all their expectations—or your own. You are worn out from living life as though every appointment is an audition. Stop listening to the many voices pulling at you. Listen instead to My voice. Come to Me. Let Me help you dig up the old foundation. Find your significance in Me. I offer all the approval for which you are longing. I am not demanding. My yoke is easy (see Matthew 11:28-30). I don't have nearly the expectations for you that others have. Only in Me can you find unconditional approval. Receive My grace and allow it to become the foundation for your self-worth.

Praying Scripture to Internalize Grace

Lord, You have promised to be the sure foundation of my life (see Isaiah 33:3). Give me the Spirit of wisdom and revelation so that I might know You better and build my life around You alone. I pray that the eyes of my heart would be enlightened so that I would know the hope to which You have called me (see Ephesians 1:17-18). Show me the times when I chase after the approval of others. Reveal to me where I have sought to build my identity or find my significance in the approval of others or my own abilities. Teach me to ask myself like the apostle Paul did, "Am I now trying to win the approval of men, or of God? Or am I trying to please men?" (Galatians 1:10).

Holy Spirit, convict me that chasing the approval of others is meaningless, like chasing after the wind (see Ecclesiastes 2:17). Instead, let me root the core of who I am in Your grace. Thank You that I am completely known, loved, forgiven, empowered, and pursued by You.

Thank You, Lord, that You don't judge me by external appearances (see Galatians 2:6). Instead, You see my heart and You love me just the same. Thank You that I am not justified by how well I obey the rules but rather I am declared righteous because of Your grace, and Your grace alone (see Galatians 2:16). Thank You that I don't need the justification of others because I have been justified freely by Your grace through the redemption that is in Christ Jesus (see Romans 3:24). I thank You that You give me Your Spirit. He is the One who transforms me. Help me not to go backward and try to attain spirituality by human effort (see Galatians 3:4).

Your Word tells me You reached out to me because of Your kindness and love and that You saved me not because of the righteous things I had done or because of how well I performed but because of Your mercy. My hope is in Your grace (see Titus 3:4-7). Thank You for Your unconditional acceptance.

A Daily Dose of Grace

Day 1

1. Memorize and meditate on Ephesians 1:3-6 as written here or in another translation:

> Praise be to the God and Father of our Lord Jesus Christ, who has blessed us in the heavenly realms with every spiritual blessing in Christ. For he chose us in him before the creation of the world to be holy and blameless in his sight. In love he predestined us to be adopted as his sons through Jesus Christ, in accordance with his pleasure and will—to the praise of his glorious grace, which he has freely given us in the One he loves.

2. What does Ephesians 1:3-6 teach about your identity?

3. We summarized Christ's core message as being a message of grace. In your own words, describe how Jesus Christ is living proof of God's grace.

Day 2

1. Read Ephesians 1:11-12. How does being "in Christ" provide a sure foundation for your identity? (*Predestined* is another way of saying that we were chosen. Don't be intimidated by that word.) As children, we dreaded being chosen last for teams. How does it make you feel that you were chosen by God?

2. Read Ephesians 1:13-14. What two word pictures do these verses give us for the Holy Spirit? How does the indwelling Holy Spirit reassure our hearts that we belong to God?

3. Read Romans 8:28-29. What promise is given to those who are in Christ? How does this promise shape our identities?

Day 3

1. The apostle John defined himself as "the disciple whom Jesus loved" (John 13:23). Take an honest look at your life. How have you tried to build your identity apart from being loved by Christ (for example, career, relationships, and so on)?

2. Following are eight aspects of a woman's life. Look them over and then write one or two sentences under each aspect. Describe the expectations you experience in that aspect of your life. Then describe how that aspect of your life would look if you internalized grace.

a. Spiritual

b. Familial

c. Vocational

d. Intellectual

e. Emotional

f. Physical

g. Social

h. Missional

Day 4

1. Read John 15:9-11. How can abiding in Christ help strengthen your confidence in God's grace?

2. Read 2 Corinthians 5:5-8. How does the Holy Spirit build confidence in our hearts?

3. Read Leviticus 26:13. How can living up to the expectations of others put you in bondage? Every relationship will carry with it some level of expectations. How do you decide which expectations are realistic and which are not? How does God's grace allow us to let go of the unrealistic expectations of others and hold our heads high?

Day 5

1. When you are strengthening your core and deciding which expectations are realistic and which are not, it can be helpful to analyze your core beliefs, core values, and core life message. To help you do this, list your core beliefs and core values. Then write a statement describing your core life message.

   a. Core Beliefs

   b. Core Values

   c. Core Life Message

Day 6

1. Review Ephesians 1:3-6.

2. What have you learned about yourself in this chapter? What have you learned about grace?

3. Wear a bracelet today. Every time you look at that bracelet, remind yourself that you are fully known, loved, forgiven, empowered, and pursued by God. Your core identity is founded in that truth. You are the disciple who Jesus loves. You don't need to try to find your identity in your job, your husband, your children, your friends, or any other relationship.

CHAPTER 4

Give Yourself Permission to Rest

We must drink deeply from the very Source of deep calm and peace of interior quietude and refreshment of God, allowing the pure water of divine grace to flow plentifully from the Source itself.

Mother Teresa

The sound of the phone ringing jolted me out of a dead sleep. The voice on the other end of the line said, "Hi, Becky. This is Lois. I just wanted to let you know that I am downstairs waiting in the lobby to pick you up and take you to the conference."

For one brief, disoriented moment, I couldn't remember where I was, who Lois was, or why she was calling me. Then it hit me like a splash of ice-cold water thrown directly between my eyes: I had overslept.

I couldn't believe it. I *never* oversleep. But sure enough, I checked the hotel clock, and to my horror it read 7:50 a.m.—the exact time Lois had said she would pick me up. I was supposed to teach four sessions at her church that morning. The alarm had not gone off, and now she was waiting downstairs in the lobby.

I bolted out of bed, unable to decide what to do first. Brush my teeth? Put on my makeup? Do my hair? What had I planned to wear, and where were my notes? I made it downstairs in seven minutes. (Please be impressed.) And, by the grace of God alone, I think I even made sense teaching all day.

Later that night on my flight home, I reflected on the weeks and even months prior to the conference. I realized that I had unconsciously allowed my schedule to become too full. That's a nice way of saying I was riding through life at breakneck speed, stressed out, and slightly spastic, a common problem for us performers.

I have been mulling this over in my mind, trying to figure out what sucks us into a whirlwind of busyness, and have come up with a few culprits:

- **The never-ending to-do list.** If I don't do it, who will?
- **The pressure to produce.** Productivity feeds our insatiable appetite to accomplish and succeed. But when is enough enough, and who defines success?
- **The quest for financial security.** Many women work more than forty hours a week in order to make ends meet, but at what cost?
- **Our addiction to applause.** A full calendar feeds our egos. After all, if my calendar is full, I must be important, right?

We performers take on too much and end up stressed out. Perhaps you are longing for a vacation right now! Your to-do list is extensive, there aren't enough hours in the day, and life feels overwhelming. Your spiritual walk is limping. Who has time for soul care? Sigh.

I imagine that some of the people who followed Jesus, including the twelve disciples, felt maxed out at times as well. Jesus looked out into the hearts of the exhausted and depleted and told a tiny parable with big implications for the tired performer.

THE PARABLE OF THE GROWING SEED

This is the story He told:

> This is what the kingdom of God is like. A man scatters seed on the ground. Night and day, whether he sleeps or gets up, the seed sprouts and grows, though he does not know how. All by itself the soil produces grain—first the stalk, then the head, then the full kernel in the head. As soon as the grain is ripe, he puts the sickle to it, because the harvest has come. (Mark 4:26-29)

When I noticed a particular sentence in this story, I practically danced. Can you guess which one? If you guessed, "Night and day, whether he sleeps or gets up, the seed sprouts and grows, though he does not know how" (verse 27), you are right. In the previous verse, the farmer scatters the seed; this is his responsibility. But then he goes to sleep, and the next day he goes about his business. He rests and then goes back to work. Meanwhile, the seed sprouts and grows, even while the farmer is resting.

In all my years as a student of the Bible, I had missed this one statement. I heard many sermons that taught that if I didn't share Jesus enough, people would go to hell. I imagined my friends crying out, "Becky, why didn't you convince me?" When I was five years old, I told my best friend she was going to hell because she didn't know Jesus. None too thrilled, her mom called mine, warning that if I kept talking about hell, Anna and I would not be able to play together.

My angst continued even as an adult. I felt burdened to change the world. I accepted any ministry opportunity that came to me, at times ignoring my own needs for soul care. Requests from my children's schools also burdened me. After all, as a Christ follower, shouldn't I make every effort to be involved and influence my community for Christ? I felt unsure about where to draw the line, uncertain of what was God's part in ministry and what was mine.

Now, don't get me wrong. Has God called us to share how Christ's saving grace has changed our lives? Absolutely. For sure. But He hasn't called us to save the entire world. A driven lifestyle is never of God. It is the result of human effort. I like how Charles Swindoll puts it: "Religion says, Work more, try harder. Do this. Don't do that. Give until you have no more. God isn't yet pleased with you. Push, push harder, longer. Jesus looked into the heart of exhausted, overburdened, anxious, stressed-out people and offered a better way."[1]

GRACE GLIMPSE

Grace invites me to a balanced lifestyle that includes both work and rest.

Jesus on Rest

Jesus had quite a bit to say about rest. He said, "Come to me, all you who are weary and burdened, and I will give you rest" (Matthew 11:28). In the New Testament, the word *rest* comes from the Greek word *anapausis*, which means "cessation, refreshment."[2] It is closely related to the Hebrew word for Sabbath. God instituted the idea of Sabbath rest from the beginning. After working to create the world for six days, He rested on the seventh. He told Moses that the seventh day of every week was to be set aside as the Sabbath. On that day, the Israelites were not to do any work; they were to rest and find refreshment in God alone (see Exodus 20:10-11). Did you catch the rhythm there? God worked, and then He rested.

Jesus went on to say, "Take my yoke upon you and learn from me, for I am gentle and humble in heart, and you will find rest for your souls. For my yoke is easy and my burden is light" (11:29-30). At the time of Christ, a rabbi's teaching was called a yoke. Many of these yokes felt heavy because the rabbis called their followers to perform at such a high standard. In fact, Jewish boys studied the Torah (the first five books of the Old Testament) until they were twelve, when they were tested to see if they had memorized all of Genesis, Exodus, Leviticus, Numbers, and Deuteronomy. If a boy performed well, he could continue his studies; if not, he was invited to take up a trade. Those who continued memorized the rest of the Old Testament. When a boy turned sixteen, he approached the rabbi of his choice to ask to be accepted as a disciple. Once accepted, a disciple would take that rabbi's yoke (teaching and interpretation of Scriptures) upon himself.[3] The entire system of discipleship was based on performance.

Not so with Jesus. The prophet Isaiah tells us that Jesus came to shatter the old yoke (see Isaiah 9:4). Throughout His earthly ministry, He invited His followers to "come with [Him] by yourselves to a quiet place and get some rest" (Mark 6:31). That invitation was not just for His followers then; it is for us today as well.

We live in a society that glorifies busyness and rewards productivity. Many of us are living on overload. We want to do more and be more; our lives are so full we have no margin for rest. We forget that although God ordained work, He also ordained rest. He values our being *with* Him as much or even more than our doing *for* Him. He invites us to come to Him and receive His rest.

Here's what I believe He meant: Rest is relaxing, letting go of cares, and experiencing refreshment from God. This is the idea behind Psalm 131:2. David wrote, "I have stilled and quieted my soul; like a weaned child with its mother, like a weaned child is my soul within me." A toddler who has grown beyond the need of breast milk doesn't keep crying out to be nursed. She lets go and relaxes against her mother's breast and gives in to the rest for which she is longing.

Sinking into grace allows us to rest, to understand that we don't have to do it all, that it's okay to let go and recharge. We can trust that God's Spirit is at work, causing "the seeds" to grow while we rest.

Jesus modeled this. Throughout the Gospels, He healed the sick, raised the dead, and challenged the legalism of the Pharisees. But then He withdrew, seeking solitude and silence with the Father in order to recharge. We see an example of this in Mark 1:35-38. Jesus was spending time alone with His Father. The day before had been a busy day of healing the sick and casting out demons. It was early in the morning, still dark outside, and Jesus was praying. All of a sudden, some frazzled disciples interrupted His quiet, saying, "Everyone is looking for you!" (verse 37). (You gotta love it. Jesus is God. Don't you think He could manage His own schedule? Yet the disciples reminded Him of all the people waiting to be healed.) Jesus didn't allow Himself to feel pressured; instead, He told the disciples it was time to leave and go to a different village to minister.

What Jesus modeled here has profound implications for the performer. *Jesus didn't heal everyone.* He didn't say yes to every need. Instead, He took care of His own soul needs and spent uninterrupted times of communion with the Father. He modeled the rhythm of grace: work balanced with rest.

Jesus needed to escape the chaos of life and find rest with God, and so do we. Yet many of us are reluctant to rest. The feeling of being needed makes us feel important, valuable. We like to feel that God *needs* us to change the world for Him. That was the prophet Elijah's problem.

Slow Down Before You Burn Out

We find the story in 1 Kings 18–19. Elijah had been ministering and prophesying full-time, nonstop. Not an easy job when your prophesying includes rebukes for King Ahab and his wicked wife, Jezebel. The king and Jezebel had been leading God's people into Baal worship, so Elijah challenged the prophets of Baal to a showdown of power on Mount Carmel. Elijah told the people to lay out two sacrifices and call on Baal to rain down fire and consume one of the sacrifices. He said that he would also call on his God, Jehovah, to rain down fire and consume the other sacrifice. Whichever deity answered would be declared the one true God.

God honored Elijah's prayer and consumed the sacrifice with fire that fell from the heavens. After the huge fireworks show, Elijah had all four hundred prophets of Baal killed. He then ran all the way to Jezerel, which was miles away.

Now, you would think Elijah would be on a spiritual mountaintop. The problem was, Jezebel vowed to have Elijah hunted down and killed. After what Elijah had witnessed on Mount Carmel, you would think her threat would not have rattled him. But Scripture tells us that Elijah ran away, curled up under a broom tree, and asked God to take his life just a few hours after God's awesome display of power.

Elijah was physically, emotionally, and spiritually exhausted. If we take a closer look at what led to his burnout, we discover that Elijah had begun to believe a subtle lie: *I am indispensable to God's work.* He told God, "I am the only one left" (19:10). Elijah had fallen victim to the lie that so many leaders and doers fall into: *It's all up to me. If I don't do it, it won't get done.* Gradually, we begin to think we are indispensable. When that attitude creeps in, burnout is right around the corner.

My friend, God invites you to share His grace with others and join His mission in the world, but you live in a human body, and like it or not, you need rest. Let me share with you some things that have helped me find the rhythm that Jesus modeled between work and rest, between doing and being.

Doing, Grace Style

These are guidelines that have helped me have a grace-based approach to work and ministry. You don't need to do them all. Just try one and see if it helps you embrace the rhythm of grace.

Respond to the movement of the Holy Spirit, not to every whim of your heart. Rather than trying to meet all the needs out there, depend on the Holy Spirit to guide you to those He wants you to do something about.

The prophet Ezekiel did this. He had a vision in which he saw creatures with a wheel next to each one. The wheels sparkled and looked just alike. Ezekiel wrote, "Wherever the spirit would go, they would go" (1:20). What if our days began with this prayer? *Holy Spirit, I only want to move with You today. Wherever You move, that's where I want to move. My desire is to flow in sync with You today.* I am guessing we would experience far less stress, because the Holy Spirit is never stressed and He does not lead us to a driven lifestyle.

Later in that same passage, Ezekiel falls on his face before the Lord (see 1:28-2:2). God calls Ezekiel to his feet and sends the Spirit into him to provide the energy for him to rise to his feet. Ezekiel wrote, "The Spirit came into me and raised me" (2:2). Oh, I love that. The Holy Spirit raised Ezekiel up. Are you feeling too tired to get up and do what God is asking of you? Do you feel too exhausted to move? Respond only to the movement of the Spirit. What God calls you to do, the Holy Spirit will provide the energy for. He will raise you up! And while you rest, the Spirit will continue to grow the seeds you have planted.

Set boundaries and don't step beyond them. Understand what you can and can't do. Nancie Carmichael, whom I quoted in the previous chapter, describes a time in her life when her quest to do it all left her exhausted and with a diagnosis of fibromyalgia. She wrote, "Something was wrong here. Early in life, I'd learned that good performance equals acceptance with God. . . . The doctor's words echoed in my mind: 'Do you have to do so much? Who do you think you are, Wonder Woman?'"[4]

Performers who don't understand boundaries try to be superhuman. When we set boundaries, we are saying that we can't do it all and we can trust God and others to do what we can't. Boundaries are the limits we set for ourselves. They help us identify what is our responsibility and what responsibilities belong to others. Establishing boundaries is a way of honoring our God-given limits. The woman who does not learn to set boundaries will be overwhelmed on a daily basis. If that's you, it's time to get alone with God and do some reflective thinking. Take a look at your life. What needs to change in order for you to feel calmer and more in control? Where do you need to set firmer limits? What might God be calling you to let go of?

When new opportunities come, don't immediately say yes. When you wait and pray before you accept new responsibilities, you have time to ask yourself such questions as *Is this opportunity something I feel passionate about? Is it something that will allow me to use my gifts? What is the time commitment? Am I saying yes because I am afraid of disappointing the person who asked?* (If I am, that's a signal that I am back in performer mode and craving approval.) After you have asked these questions, seek God and ask Him what His will is before responding.

Plant seeds, don't preach. When you are developing relationships in order to share Christ, plant seeds of grace. Don't use a lot of words. As performers who desire to change the world, we often talk too much. This is especially true if our lives are full and we are in a rush. We feel we have a set amount of time and must make the most of every opportunity, but as a result, we can put off someone who doesn't yet know Christ. No one wants to go out for coffee and end up hearing a sermon; he or she might merely want you to listen. Planting a seed might mean simply offering empathy or offering to pray with someone. It might mean asking a pointed question designed to get the other person to think. It might mean showing that person Christ's love. Or it might mean watching our tone or our facial expressions so that we don't come across as condescending while we're sharing the message of grace with someone.

Nurture relationships; don't view people as projects. It is not our job to fix people. That's God's job. Our job is to plant seeds by loving people. Every single person on this planet is a person whom God created. Each one has a story, and each one has intrinsic value and is worth knowing simply because he or she is made in the image of God. While we can't sustain relationships with everyone, we can nurture the relationships God brings across our paths.

That's what Ron Hall did. Rather than seeking to solve the entire homeless problem, Ron realized the difference he could make in investing in one relationship. In the book *Same Kind of Different as Me*, authors Ron Hall and Denver Moore describe their unique friendship. Ron Hall was an affluent art dealer, and Denver was a homeless man who had grown up on a cotton plantation and never learned to read or write. At first Ron saw Denver as a homeless person he could help. But God had other plans. Instead of "fixing" Denver's life, Ron became his friend. One of the most touching moments in their unique journey is when Denver says to Ron, "If you is lookin' for a *real* friend, then I'll be one Forever"[5]—in essence saying, "I don't want you just to invest in me. I don't want you to try to get me off the streets. I just want a forever friendship."

When we let go of our compulsion to fix everyone, it is far easier to take time for the rest Christ offers.

Taking Time for Rest

Rest involves the practices of self-care, sanctuary, Sabbath, and savoring the moment.

The Practice of Self-Care

Self-care means becoming intentional about taking care of one's body, soul, and spirit. It includes such things as exercise, healthful eating, recreation, regular visits to the doctor, and activities that rejuvenate. Some women find that going for a massage, facial, manicure, or pedicure rejuvenates them. Self-care might mean taking care of your emotional health by talking with a counselor, or perhaps it includes setting firmer boundaries so that you have space in your schedule to reflect on your life and what God is doing. It might be that you need to make the time to schedule your mammogram. Women who practice self-care are usually better able to take care of the needs of others.

TIPS FOR SELF-CARE

Rest—Psalm 23:2
Reflection—Psalm 48:9
Recreation—Philippians 3:1
Prayer—Luke 5:16; Philippians 4:6
Physical exercise—1 Corinthians 9:27
Physical pampering (massage, facial, haircut)—1 Corinthians 6:20
Silence and solitude—1 Kings 19:12
Singing—Psalm 30:4
Spiritual friendship—John 15:12

The Practice of Sanctuary

Because the spirit of Jesus Christ lives within us (see 1 Corinthians 6:15), we need to be intentional about spending time with God in order to experience His rest. The practice of sanctuary involves intentionally setting aside time and space to connect with God, engaging in what some have called the spiritual disciplines, such as Bible reading, prayer, meditation, and memorization.

Part of my fear in writing this book is that readers will think I am saying, "Chill about your Christian walk. Don't worry about the spiritual disciplines." That is *not* what I am saying. My point is that we don't practice the spiritual disciplines to earn approval from God; we practice them to mature in our walk with God. If you internalize grace, you'll want to engage with God and spend time with Him. The practice of sanctuary keeps us disciplined about spending time with God and keeps our souls awake to the presence of God.

Every morning I meet with God at 5:30. I often begin this time on my knees in front of a white comfy chair in my office, worshipping and praising God. Then I sit in the chair and spend time reading my Bible, journaling, praying, and listening for God's voice. I express my desire to live in union with Jesus Christ. Sometimes I practice centering prayer during this time. Author Judith Hougen wrote, "Centering prayer is a time of extended contemplation." She goes on to describe centering prayer as "a quiet, loving gaze"[6] on Christ. During centering prayer, we sit with Christ in stillness, as if we have a deep, abiding intimacy. There is not a need for words. In the silence, we find rest and refreshment. That's why the psalmist wrote, "Be still, and know that I am God" (Psalm 46:10).

In centering prayer, we direct our full attention on our Lord. Many of us have trouble focusing, and that can feel frustrating. Judith Hougen writes, "It is like sitting in the most beautiful cathedral ever built but only noticing the fly that's buzzing near you."[7] As we learn to intentionally take every thought captive (see 2 Corinthians 10:5) and turn each thought back to God, we are more able to direct our full attention to Him. It takes time and practice to learn to focus, so be patient with yourself. One way to focus our attention on Him is to choose a prayer word or phrase before we start. When our thoughts become distracted, we can use that word to bring our focus back to the Lord. Sometimes when my thoughts wander, I bring my attention back by whispering, "Abba." Or, I pray, *My Beloved, let me rest in You*. With practice, centering prayer becomes easier and ultimately we find rest in heart-to-heart communion with our Lord.

SUGGESTIONS FOR SANCTUARY TIME

Create a time and place to regularly meet with God.
Light a candle.
Listen to worship music.
Practice silence and listening to God.
Underline and mark with a date verses that speak to you personally.
Use a list of the names of God for your praise time.

Practice centering prayer.
Take a prayer walk.
Focus on one portion of Scripture.
Use a devotional book, such as Ruth Myers' The Satisfied Heart *or* 31 Days of Praise.
Use a journal and write out your prayers as if they were letters to God.

The Practice of Sabbath

I have heard some say this practice is not for today. I disagree. The principle of Sabbath rest is repeated throughout Scripture and is offered as a gift of God's grace. In the New Testament, the author of Hebrews wrote, "There remains, then, a Sabbath-rest for the people of God; for anyone who enters God's rest also rests from his own work, just as God did from his. Let us, therefore, make every effort to enter that rest" (4:9-11). When Jesus came, He challenged the Pharisees' legalistic teachings about the Sabbath so that His followers would understand that the Sabbath was given as a restorative gift in order for the people of God to remember what life was about. The Jewish Sabbath began in the evening when the family set aside all work. The goal was to settle into the peace and calm of the Sabbath. Upon waking the next morning, they were to celebrate and delight in the friendship they had with God.

Today we can practice the Sabbath by purposely and regularly, perhaps once a week, withdrawing from normal activities for the purpose of rest and worship. The culture in which we live screams against this purposeful withdrawal. We are constantly bombarded with demands and messages. Our technology gives us round-the-clock accessibility to work and deadlines. But God has made our bodies with limits, and He provided the Sabbath so that we can find refreshment and renewal in Him.

Although Sundays are busy for me because my husband, Steve, is a pastor, I still try to practice a form of Sabbath rest that day. We attend church and then often enjoy lunch with our kids and grandkids. Then, after Sunday dinner, sometimes I curl up with a good book. Steve often takes a nap. We may relax with a ball game or take a hike. The key is to engage in activities that rest and refresh you.

Another way I practice Sabbath rest is to regularly withdraw from daily activity by taking a day of prayer once a month. I fast from e-mail and spend leisurely time reading my Bible, journaling, and worshipping. I take walks and simply commune with the Lord. I have found these prayer days essential for providing a sense of renewal in my life.

The Practice of Rest in the Moment

If your mind is like mine, it has about ten thousand thoughts per minute. Sometimes I need a vacation from my thoughts. Let's look at some practical ways to find rest in the moment.

Discover the joy of inward retreats. I have discovered that I can pull away at any moment, no matter where I am, for a mini-retreat of the soul.

Madame Jeanne Guyon was a French author during the 1600s who wrote about experiencing God's presence. She spoke of taking a "gentle retreat inward to a present God."[8] I have tried this and have found myself refreshed in God's presence. When I feel frazzled or frantic, I stop and ask the Holy Spirit to refill my life with His peace. I ask Him to remind me of His presence, and I praise Him that He lives within. I whisper how much I love Him and ask Him to live His life through me.

When I am intentional about turning inward to His presence, God faithfully reassures me that I am fully known, loved, forgiven, empowered, and pursued by Him. I can rest in this truth. You can too. When you feel as though the pressure is too much and you might explode, turn inward to the Spirit of Christ, who dwells in you. Ask Him to quiet your soul and reassure you of your significance in Him.

Exhale stress and inhale the breath of the Holy Spirit. During an especially stressful time, I learned how to practice a new type of spiritual breathing. Our youngest daughter had just graduated from high school, and two weeks later her sister was getting married. My life became a hubbub of details. I wanted to enjoy both events but felt stressed and tense.

One morning before anyone else was up, I came across a reading by Isaac Penington called "Waiting for Breathings from His Spirit." Intrigued, I began to read. Isaac was a Quaker who lived between 1617–1680. While in prison for his faith, he wrote, "Therefore, we ought to wait diligently for the leadings of the Holy Spirit in everything we do. . . . O Friend, do you not have a sense of the way to the Father? Then you must press your spirit to bow daily before God and wait for breathings to you from his Spirit."[9] The morning I read this, I was feeling anxious about all that I had to accomplish. I got down on my knees and visualized myself exhaling all the stress and tension I was holding in my body. Then I spoke softly to the Holy Spirit, asking Him to refill my lungs with His breath. Almost immediately, I felt a peace that passes human understanding. Since that time, I have been practicing this form of breathing: exhaling my stress and inhaling the Holy Spirit's peace. When I do this, my soul is instantly refreshed.

Eliminate rushing, embrace transition time. In order to experience the rest that Christ offers, give yourself some time and space between events and meetings, and use that time to get centered. For example, if you've had a stressful appointment with a client, close your door and give yourself three to five minutes of transition time. Give the anxiety of the last appointment to the Lord. Lay every worry at His feet, and then ask the Holy Spirit to refill your spirit with His energy.

If your family needs you the moment you walk in the door after work, use your car time as a transition time. Drive for a few minutes in absolute silence. Visualize leaving all your work worries at the office. Then spend some time listening to worship music and ask the Lord to prepare you for what lies at home.

I began this practice years ago, when my children were small.

About twenty minutes before Steve got home from work, I began praying that the Lord would enable me to fully engage with my husband. I prayed that I would listen well and show interest in his day—that I would ask questions and be able to show him how much I cared about his world. Some days this was difficult, particularly if it had been a rough day with our kids. But I found that the effort was well worth it because I learned to flow through my day more peacefully and less stressed out.

I find that after I have spent significant time resting and being with God, my soul is regenerated and I reengage with the right motive. I am able to serve God and others out of love rather than because I need an ego fix.

Let Go

When my kids were toddlers, life felt like constant activity. Evening would come and I would bathe them, feed them a bedtime snack, read to them, and pray over them. By that time, I was ready for bed. But often they were not, and although they were tired, they would fight sleep as hard as they could. On particularly difficult nights, I would hold them, walk back and forth, and sing over them, stroking their hair as they wiggled and squirmed in my arms, trying to keep their eyes open. If I was patient, eventually I felt their tiny bodies go limp with sleep.

Some of us are like toddlers. We wiggle and squirm in the arms of God. He invites us to rest, but we keep going and fight to do more. God offers to hold us in His arms. He longs to stroke our souls and tell us how much He loves us. Rather than fight Him, why not let go? Sink into His loving, gracious arms and find the refreshment He is longing to give you.

Message from the Grace Giver

Precious one, I long to restore your soul (see Psalm 23:2). The world has warped your thinking into believing that you must be busy to be valuable. Subconsciously, you feel guilty for stopping to rest. Come with Me, by yourself, to a quiet place and get some rest (see Mark 6:31). Let me refresh you, body, soul, and spirit. Be still (see Psalm 46:10). Don't rush your time with Me. Linger and allow My Spirit to renew you. Your to-do list will always seem vitally important, but achievement will never fill the deepest ache in your heart. Only My loving presence can refresh your soul.

Praying Scripture to Internalize Grace

Lord, I confess that in all my striving to perform, I have lost sight of rest. Your Word tells me that there remains a Sabbath rest for the people of God, for anyone who enters God's rest also rests from his own work (see Hebrews 4:9). Rest was Your idea (see Hebrews 4:9; Genesis 2:2). You promise to "lead me beside quiet waters and restore my soul" (see Psalm 23:2-3). You promise rest when I choose the right path for my life (see Jeremiah 6:16). Help me embrace rest so You can restore my soul.

When I feel spastic, frazzled, or overwhelmed, help me to mimic the self-talk of the psalmist David, who wrote, "Find rest, O my soul, in God alone; my hope comes from him" (Psalm 62:5). Your Word teaches me that she "who dwells in the shelter of the Most High will rest in the shadow of the Almighty" (91:1). The more I live moment by moment in Your presence, the more I experience the rest and refreshment You promise. My heart cries out, "How lovely is your dwelling place, O Lord Almighty!" (84:1). Thank You that my strength is in You (see verse 7).

Jesus, the pattern of Your life was to withdraw to lonely places and pray (see Luke 5:16). You prioritized time with Your Father. Teach me to do the same. When everyone seems to want a piece of me, help me to hear the soft whisper of Your voice, inviting me to come with You to a quiet place and get some rest (see Mark 6:31). How I praise You that You offer this promise: "Come to me, all you who are weary and burdened, and I will give you rest. Take my yoke upon you and learn from me . . . and you will find rest for your souls" (Matthew 11:28-29).

A Daily Dose of Grace

Day 1

1. Memorize and meditate on Psalm 62:5 as written here or in another translation:

    > Find rest, O my soul, in God alone; my hope comes from him. He alone is my rock and my salvation; he is my fortress, I will not be shaken.

2. What does it mean to you personally that God is your rock and your fortress? How do those pictures of God help you find rest in Him?

3. Now read all of Psalm 62. What principles of rest do you see in this psalm?

Day 2

1. Read Mark 2:23–3:6 and Hebrews 4:9-10. The principle of the Sabbath was established under Old Testament law so that Jewish people would have a day to rest from work. Do you think we should practice Sabbath rest today? Why, or why not?

2. Read Mark 1:29-38. How did Jesus model the rhythm of grace? How can the expectations of others push us to a driven lifestyle? How did Jesus handle the expectations of the disciples?

Day 3

1. Read Psalm 91:1-5 and then answer the following questions:
   a. What do these verses teach us about rest?

   b. How can God's presence be a shelter to you in the midst of a chaotic day?

c. In verse 4, the psalmist speaks of God's faithfulness being a shield and rampart. Those words speak of protection. How does God's faithfulness provide protection for you?

Day 4

1. Read Psalm 131. Write your own definition of *rest* based on this psalm. Would you describe yourself as having a stilled and quieted soul? Why, or why not? Describe what rest feels like to you.

2. Read Zephaniah 3:17. Are you comfortable with silence? Why, or why not? What does it look like for the Lord to quiet you with His love? How do you prevent Him from quieting you with His love? What has He spoken to you through this verse?

Day 5

1. Read Psalm 84 and then answer the following questions:
   a. What principles of rest and renewal do you see in this psalm?

   b. Do you feel guilty for "wasting time in God's presence"? Where does that feeling of guilt come from? How could setting aside a specific time and place to spend time with God help your feelings of guilt?

   c. What practical steps do you see in this psalm for cultivating a sense of God's presence throughout the day?

   d. What would prevent you from taking those steps?

   e. How can resting increase your strength?

Day 6

1. Review Psalm 62:5.

2. Is it easier for you to serve the Lord or love the Lord? What messages did you receive in childhood about "doing" for God? How have those messages impacted your ability to rest?

3. What change will you make in your life this week so that you can spend time resting with the Lord? Make a plan to spend a half day intentionally resting with the Lord. Your plan can include such things as prayer, a hike, a bike ride, a walk on the beach, a massage, a picnic, time reading your Bible and journaling, and time listening to music. Whatever you do, spend time talking with and listening to God.

4. Sometime in the next week, practice centering prayer. Write about your experience in the space provided.

CHAPTER 5

Find Your Purpose and Passion

Recognizing who we are in Christ and aligning our life with God's purpose for us gives us a sense of destiny. . . . It gives form and direction to our life.

Jean Fleming

Many performers fail to get on the unique path God has called them to and consequently end up feeling empty, lost, and purposeless. That was true for Kathy. She wrote,

> I had this sense that when people were demanding or expecting something from me, especially if they were ungraceful about it, somebody had to have grace, and that someone would be me. I would do everything in my power to respond and behave graciously and gracefully, even if it killed me. I gave and went the extra mile over and over until I became physically ill in the process, developing Addison's disease. That means I don't deal with stress well because I exhausted my adrenal glands. Now I find that if someone places an expectation on me, I literally cannot respond. I just physically can't do it without it putting me in bed for several days.

> Slowly, I am finding what inspires me and what drains me—or *who* inspires or drains. And I'm beginning to find out who I am, what I want to do, and that sometimes grace is not jumping in to fix something but just caring about the person.

Like Kathy, many women live without a clear sense of purpose. They may have full, active lives but lack a sense of fulfillment. Why? Because we were created to glorify God and need a cause bigger than ourselves.

Until we discover what that looks like, we may wonder, *Why am I here?* Many women revisit this question throughout the changing seasons of their lives. Natalie wonders, *Will my life ever matter for more than diaper changing?* As Marcy sits at her desk entering numbers into her computer at her work cubicle, she wonders, *Is this all there is to life?* Sandy has just sent her last child off to college. Her home feels quiet and empty, and her heart cries, *What's next? My whole life has been wrapped up in raising kids. I don't feel as if I know who I am.* We long to know if our lives matter.

If you wonder the same thing, I want to tell you a simple story Jesus told.

The Parable of a Lamp on a Stand

"No one lights a lamp and hides it in a jar or puts it under a bed. Instead, he puts it on a stand, so that those who come in can see the light" (Luke 8:16). The point? When we receive God's grace, each of us receives a divine calling and purpose. We are to be Light bearers. We are priests (see 1 Peter 2:9). As priests we have a calling on our lives to share Christ and His love with others. Our purpose is to speak and live out the message of grace to the world around us.

You may feel empty and lost right now because you are floundering between decisions, you've failed at something you thought you would succeed at, or you've made some wrong choices. But the truth is that your life matters to God. You are here for a purpose, for this time, in these circumstances because God has a plan for you.

GRACE GLIMPSE

God's grace gives purpose and meaning to my life.

A DIVINE PURPOSE, UNIQUE CALLING, AND SUPERNATURAL POWER

As pastor and author Rick Warren says, "The purpose of your life is far greater than your own personal fulfillment, your peace of mind, or even your happiness. It's far greater than your family, your career, or even your wildest dreams and ambitions. . . . You must begin with God."[1] You were created by God and for God.

What is God's plan? First, that you would live in relationship with Him for the "praise of his glory" (Ephesians 1:12). Second, that you would join Him in His mission of bringing His kingdom to earth. The apostle Paul wrote that we are "God's workmanship, created in Christ Jesus to do good works, which God prepared in advance for us to do" (Ephesians 2:10). The word *workmanship* is from the Greek word *poiema*, from which we get our English word *poem*. You are God's poetic masterpiece, and He has prepared specific acts of service for you to do. The acts of service aren't ways of earning God's favor; they are evidence of His grace in your life. When you came to Jesus Christ, you joined God in His mission to make His kingdom tangible. You can do this by serving and loving people—by giving of yourself so that others can experience the life change made possible in Jesus Christ.

When I speak of one's unique calling, I'm not talking about a career. Sometimes calling and career come together, but most Christians are not paid to live out their calling. For most of us, our career is how we earn a living and pay the bills, and our calling is the role we play in God's kingdom.

When you understand and choose to live in light of your unique design, you are living out of your true self, the self God created you to be. The great thing is, God doesn't leave you to figure this out on your own. His grace provides everything you need to make a difference. You have access to the Holy Spirit's power to help live out that calling. In chapter 2, we said that in the Bible, oil often represents the Holy Spirit. In the story of the lamp on a stand, the oil again represents the Holy Spirit. The oil allowed the lamp to burn and shed light. In our lives, it is the Holy Spirit—the living Christ within us—that enables us to live out God's grace in a dark world.

One of my favorite verses is 1 Thessalonians 5:24: "The one who calls you is faithful and he will do it." I have learned to cling to that promise. When God calls me to do something and I still feel ill-equipped despite doing all I can to prepare, I remind myself, *He is faithful; He will do it.*

Sallie will tell you that the Holy Spirit empowers us when God calls us to do something. She wrote,

> When I took on the role of interim worship director last summer on an emergency basis, I knew that God was calling me to a job bigger than I saw my abilities. In many ways, I was set up to fail. I could not meet people's expectations, and I knew it, but I trusted that God had a plan because it was clear I was the person He'd chosen to meet the need. Therefore, I knew that I only had to meet God's expectations and that any other failure wouldn't matter. As I have worked my way through the year, I've learned a lot about who I am. I've learned what I can't do and how to tell people that. I've also learned that I can do far more than I thought I could do, with the Holy Spirit's help.

Please note that God does not promise to empower us for the things He has not called us to do. I learned this the hard way. When

Steve and I were first married, he thought I was Superwoman. One night at a church business meeting that I was unable to attend, he had me voted in as the assistant organist. This would have been fine had I known how to play the organ, but I had never touched that instrument. I felt too embarrassed to admit that I didn't know how to play the organ, so until the day we left that church, I was listed as the assistant organist. I prayed every Sunday that the church organist, who was eighty-six years old, would not get sick, let alone die. Now that I've grown up some, when I am asked to do something, I say, "I need a day to think and pray about this opportunity." Too often, in my exuberance, I have volunteered to do something I was not designed to do. This only leads to frustration and disappointment.

God made us with characteristics uniquely our own, and He is the one who provides the vision for our lives. Others, though well-meaning, cannot map out a life vision for our lives. Only God can set our course. When we live out of our own unique design, we live according to the course He has laid out and thus find meaning and purpose. We have a divine sense of direction keeping us on track with who God has called us to be.

So if God has called us and equipped us to let His light shine in a dark world, why aren't more of us living lives of purpose and passion?

WHAT KEEPS US FROM FINDING OUR UNIQUE CALLING?

Most performers I know become distracted from living with passion and purpose for one or more of the following reasons:

Trying to please others. I read recently that "to the dancers of the New York City Ballet Company, the late George Balanchine was both director and audience. They so loved, esteemed, and feared him that no matter how large the crowds, they danced for only one audience: Mr. B."[2] There will always be other dancers. If I am going to live my life with purpose and passion, I must allow Jesus Christ to become my director and audience. I must allow Him and only Him to choreograph the movements of my life.

Seeking greatness. Baruch, an assistant to the prophet Jeremiah, wrote down the prophecies that Jeremiah dictated. His job was not impressive, but it was important just the same. However, Baruch must have craved bigger opportunities, because Jeremiah told him, "Should you then seek great things for yourself? Seek them not" (Jeremiah 45:5).

When I seek the biggest and the best, I can miss extraordinary opportunities right in front of me, such as sharing Christ with a neighbor, bringing food to a sick friend, rocking a crying baby for a stressed-out young mom, or listening to the barista at Starbucks who is having a bad day. Don't underestimate the significance of the small things. It's possible that those are the best ways to let our light shine.

My friend Carol understands this. When she discovered that many of her elderly neighbors had difficulty cooking and running errands, she asked God how she could show them His love and grace. Carol began cooking meals for her neighbors and taking them to the doctor and running errands for them. What began as a small service project grew into an ongoing ministry. Carol is the Mother Teresa of her neighborhood. She demonstrates God's grace and love to one neighbor at a time. Slowly, she is changing her neighborhood for Christ.

Being too introspective. At times, I have lost my sense of purpose because I have become morbidly introspective, analyzing how I can improve or what I can do differently. I have become paralyzed by my own inadequacies and failed to minister to those around me. In Ephesians 5:8, Paul wrote that we are to live as children of the light. The way we live as a child of the light is to continually draw attention to the Light, Jesus Christ.

As performers, we are often preoccupied with our own stuff. This makes sense. After all, we want to be the center of attention! We may be focused on getting ahead, being happy, or finding satisfaction, but when we continually look at ourselves, it's as if we are putting our light under the bed.

Or maybe we have yet to discover our unique design. For that reason, I've created an exercise for discovering one's unique calling and gifts. (Read to end of the chapter and then come back and do this exercise for day 5.)

Discovering Your Own Unique Design

Ask the Holy Spirit to lead and guide you as you work through the following questions. He will be more than happy to comply because He wants you to be all that God has called you to be.

D — **Dreams** (see Psalm 37:4). What are your dreams and desires? Often our dreams and desires are God-given.

E — **Experiences** (see 2 Corinthians 1:3-4). What experiences have shaped your life? Your life story is a powerful tool. God can redeem even the mistakes and pain by using your experiences to help another.

S — **Strengths** (see Romans 12:3). What are your strengths? Many women can name their weaknesses but have great difficulty naming their strengths. In Romans 12:3, Paul wrote, "By the grace given me I say to every one of you: Do not think of yourself more highly than you ought, but rather think of yourself with sober judgment, in accordance with the measure of faith God has given you." Paul's words mean that we are to have a sober view, or a true or honest view, of both our strengths and weaknesses. If we are focused on only our strengths, we become proud. If we focus on only our weaknesses, we live in fear.

I — **Influence** (see Ephesians 5:15-16). In what spheres do you have influence (church, work, your children's schools, halfway houses, hospitals, communities)? Part of living a life of purpose is to make the most of every opportunity that God provides.

G — Gifts (see Romans 12:6-8; Ephesians 4:7-12). What spiritual gifts do you have? God gives us gifts so that His body (the church) may be built up and strengthened. If you have never taken a spiritual gifts test, ask your pastor to recommend one. There are a number of excellent spiritual gift assessment tests available.

N — Needs (see Acts 16:9-10). What needs tug at your heart? Look at the world around you, listen to the news, and become informed.

- Many parts of the world are facing a crisis because of the HIV virus and, as a result, there are millions of orphans. Consider if there is a way you can get involved.
- Many Third World countries don't have clean water. Is there something you can do to help?
- Social service organizations in your community might be in crisis because of the amount of children they've had to remove from homes. Is there a way you can demonstrate the love of Christ to those kids?
- The rate of homelessness among teenagers is on the rise. Do you have anything to offer those teens?
- What about the refugees who have been deported to the United States? What would it look like for you to help some of the refugee families adjust to life in America while at the same time sharing the love of Christ?

I don't know what needs tug at your heart, but it's my prayer that these questions will get you thinking.

Before you get started, let me summarize how my friends Lynn and Jill answered the profile questions and their plans for how to start living life on purpose.

Lynn's Unique Design Profile

My friend Lynn is a savvy businesswoman. She designs and sews high-end purses. Her purses are beautiful, but the story of God's redemption in her life is even more beautiful. Her story includes foster care, adoption, addiction to alcohol, divorce, and other losses. When Lynn met Christ and began to internalize His grace, her life changed. Lynn recognizes that God has used her past to give her a heart for those who are hurting.

D—**Dreams.** Lynn's dream is to make a difference in the world by caring for hurting and broken women.

E—**Experiences.** As she analyzed her experiences, she realized she needed to list both the good and the bad experiences. She listed loss, addiction to drugs and alcohol, love, being a parent, adoption and foster care, and sexual promiscuity before her relationship with Jesus Christ.

S—**Strengths.** Lynn realized that God had given her boldness, compassion, kindness, and diligence. What she starts she follows through on and finishes, and she is a natural helper.

I—**Influence.** As Lynn analyzed her spheres of influence, she realized she had more influence than she'd originally thought. Because of her job, she has many connections all over the United States and influences many in the business world. She also has influence in the correctional system because she has taken in many foster care children and has cared for many who are in the Department of Corrections. Lynn also has influence in her church because she is a small-group leader and leads a group for broken women. She has influence in her family and community as well.

G—Gifts. After taking a spiritual gifts assessment, Lynn realized that her top three spiritual gifts are discernment, administration, and mercy.

N — Needs. The needs of broken women tug at Lynn's heart. These women include those who are addicted to drugs and alcohol and those who are in halfway houses and are trying to transition from life in prison to life in the free world.

Lynn's design profile summary: Completing the design profile exercise confirmed to Lynn her desire to work with broken women. It helped her see that her desires and dreams were in keeping with her gift mix and past experiences. Because Lynn had experienced a life of addiction, she felt better equipped to come alongside those struggling to break free from addiction. She began to pray that God would bring into her life those struggling with addiction, and God was more than willing. Many of the women who came in contact with Lynn began opening up to her, and she began a small group leading women through a Bible study designed to help them find life transformation.

Lynn also began exploring the possibility of working with women in halfway houses. Some of the foster children she had taken in through the years had difficulty with the law. Because of this, Lynn developed connections within the court system. She has earned the right to be heard and is respected, and so she began exploring the possibility of working with women trying to transition out of prison. Lynn and her husband, Billy, have also started a nonprofit organization called The Master's Hands, which ministers to hurting men and women.

Jill's Unique Design Profile

Jill is a single woman in her early thirties who currently works as a med/surgical float nurse in a local hospital. She has always wanted to be married and have a family, so the fact that she remains single has been a struggle. Jill realizes, however, that although God has not granted her wish to marry and have children, He has placed her in a position to love kids.

D — Dreams. Jill's dreams are to change the world by loving children, especially those who have no one else to love them and who feel they don't belong.

E — Experiences. Jill has experienced the loss of friends and family. She has traveled around the world and experienced different cultures. She worked as a nurse. She grew up in a loving, stable family. She has been rejected by men and was stalked in high school by a seventeen-year-old boy. Her experiences in the dating realm make her empathetic with young women who have experienced rejection from men or who distrust men.

S — Strengths. Jill is a helper/servant, is a good listener, and is kind and compassionate. She is able to share herself and her story with others.

I—Influence. Jill has influence in her small-group Bible study, at the hospital where she works, in her church youth group (where she volunteers), and within her family.

G—Gifts. The spiritual gifts Jill has are hospitality, shepherding, and encouragement.

N—Needs. The needs that tug at Jill's heart are children who feel unloved or like they don't belong.

Jill's design profile summary: Jill feels that part of her own unique calling is to work with children, particularly children who feel unloved. She wants to get involved in the foster care system and eventually adopt. In addition, she has a heart to work with teens who feel unloved, so she is volunteering in her church's youth group. She realized through doing this exercise that her story is a valuable tool to encourage hurting teenage girls.

Fearfully and Wonderfully Made

God has designed us to live for a cause greater than ourselves. When we fulfill His calling for our lives and live out our purpose, the world is changed and we make a difference. I love how Mother Teresa put it: "I am a little pencil in the hand of a writing God who is sending a love letter to the world."[3]

You have been fearfully and wonderfully made for the purpose of helping to express God's love to the world around you. In Psalm 139:13-15, David wrote,

> You created my inmost being:
>   you knit me together in my mother's womb.
> I praise you because I am fearfully and wonderfully made;
>   your works are wonderful,
>   I know that full well.
> My frame was not hidden from you
>   when I was made in the secret place.
> When I was woven together in the depths of the earth,
>   your eyes saw my unformed body.

Consider spending some time with God, praising Him that He has designed you with intentionality.

Message from the Grace Giver

> Keep your focus on Me, My child, and I will lead you down the paths I have chosen for you. I am the way (see John 14:6), and I have designed a unique path specifically for you. Don't become distracted by allowing others to set a vision for your life. Keep your eyes on Me, and I will guide you. Because I am the light of the world (see John 8:12) and I live in you, let Me shine out My grace through your life. Don't worry so much

2. Read 1 Peter 4:10. How could using your gift to bless others be an expression of God's grace?

Day 4

1. Read 1 Peter 2:9. What does it mean to you that you are a priest? As a priest, what is your function?

2. Read Romans 12:4-8. Why did God give each person in the body of Christ different gifts? How are those gifts an expression of His grace?

3. Read 1 Corinthians 12:7-11. According to these verses, why did God give spiritual gifts? How can your gift mix help you find your passion?

about accomplishing a lot; instead, ask Me about the plans I have for your life. Allow Me to help you understand how I designed you to join Me in making My grace tangible to those around you. Your life has purpose and meaning. I have given you a unique set of gifts to help you as you partner with Me in this great adventure. Learn to shut out the many voices who will try to set a vision for your life; instead, listen to My voice. I will set the vision and you will be able to live life with passion and purpose.

Praying Scripture to Internalize Grace

Lord, I praise You because You designed and created me on purpose: "You created my inmost being; you knit me together in my mother's womb. I praise you because I am fearfully and wonderfully made; your works [including me] are wonderful" (Psalm 139:13-14). Thank You that You have a marvelous vision for my life—that "all the days ordained for me were written in your book" (verse 16). Whatever You call me to do, You are faithful and will do any work You call me to through me (see 1 Thessalonians 5:24). I can trust You to "fulfill every good purpose" in my life. I praise You that You will be glorified in my life because of Your grace (see 2 Thessalonians 1:12).

Holy Spirit, thank You for indwelling me. Help me not to put out Your fire (see 1 Thessalonians 1:19) by becoming distracted by the demands and expectations of other people. Instead, teach me to listen for Your quiet voice in my life, leading and directing me on the path You have chosen for me. Remind me that You have called me to join You in the adventure of making Your grace tangible to the world. Teach me not to hide the light. Some will experience You only through me and my willingness to shine for You.

Teach me to listen to Your voice so that I will know who You have called me to be (see Isaiah 30:15). Let me be like young Samuel, who said, "Speak, Lord, for your servant is listening" (1 Samuel 3:9). You have promised that You will lead me besides streams of water on a level path where I will not stumble (see Jeremiah 31:9). Help me to stay on that level path and not become distracted by the demands of other people.

Help me not to frustrate Your plans for my life by attempting to do things in my own strength. I have such a tendency to try harder, but You have said, "Not by might nor by power, but by my Spirit" (Zechariah 4:6). My deepest desire is for You to live Your life through me. Lord, I pray that You, and You alone, will be my vision.

A Daily Dose of Grace

Day 1

1. Memorize and meditate on Ephesians 2:10 as written here or in another translation:

> We are God's workmanship, created in Christ Jesus to do good works, which God prepared in advance for us to do.

2. The word *workmanship* speaks to the fact that you are God's unique poem—His creative masterpiece. What prevents you from believing that you are God's masterpiece?

Day 2

1. Read the parable of the lamp on a stand (see Luke 8:16). What does this verse speak to you personally about sharing God's grace with the world around you?

2. What keeps you from sharing God's grace with others? (Rem we are to speak about and live out His grace to others.) W harder for you, speaking about His grace or living it out?

3. If someone asked you how he or she could become a follc Jesus Christ, would you know how to answer? Read over the on page 31 of chapter 2. Based on that prayer, outline wh would tell someone about receiving God's grace. If you have it won't feel as scary. For example, your plan might start like

> Everyone has done something wrong. Our wrongdoing called sin (see Romans 3:23).
> Our sin separates us from God (see Romans 6:23).

Day 3

1. Read John 4:1-26. In this passage, Jesus has a lengthy conve with the woman at the well. This woman is a beautiful pictu woman without a purpose. When she met Jesus, He offe Living Water. Do you think she discovered a new sense of pu What evidence can you find to support your opinion?

Day 5

1. Do the design profile. Then write a summary of what you learned and write out one or two tangible steps you can take to start living life on purpose.

   D—Dreams. What are your dreams and desires?

   E—Experiences. What experiences have shaped your life?

   S—Strengths. What are your strengths?

   I—Influence. In what spheres do you have influence?

   G—Gifts. What are your spiritual gifts?

   N—Needs. What are the needs that tug at your heart?

2. Write your design profile summary. Then write a prayer of praise for how God has crafted you intentionally to help express His love to the world.

Day 6

1. Review Ephesians 2:10.

2. How has this chapter helped you define your passion and purpose?

3. In one sentence, write out a purpose statement for your life.

CHAPTER 6

Put Away the Measuring Stick

Our constant propensity to compare ourselves to the women around us is wrecking our perceptions of both ourselves and them.
Beth Moore

"Miss Keri, please, please, can't I do a cartwheel in the show too?"

My daughter, who directs children's theater, sighed, her patience running low. Ten-year-old Clayton had already asked at least six times to do a cartwheel in the upcoming performance of *Peter Pan*. Keri had chosen another student, talented in acrobatics, to do a number of flying tricks in the performance. Clayton envied the other little boy and was positive his cartwheel could compete with any trick the other boy could perform. All week long, he argued, begged, and pleaded, but Keri held firm.

The night of the performance, the theater held a packed-out house of proud parents, all waiting eagerly to see their up-and-coming stars perform. Minutes before showtime, Clayton put in one more plea: "Please, Miss Keri? Please can I do a cartwheel?" Keri stood firm. No cartwheel. Clayton would have to be content with the role assigned.

About halfway through the show, Keri noticed Clayton eyeing her with a sheepish grin. Then it happened. In the middle of a very mellow scene, without warning, Clayton threw caution to the wind and ran onto the stage with all the gusto a ten-year-old boy can muster and did a less-than-perfect cartwheel.

Although I laughed at Clayton's antics when Keri told me this story, my heart goes out to him. Clayton reminds me a bit of myself. I too have longed to be in the spotlight and sometimes feel envy when I compare my talents with the gifts, achievements, and prestige that others possess.

Most performers struggle with envy, although it comes in different forms. See if you can identify with any of the following women's stories.

Julie has been begging God to bring a man into her life. She's longing to experience love and marriage. It has been tough for her to participate in a small-group Bible study at her church because she fights feelings of jealousy. The other women are happily married and have children. She told me,

> I have recently been walking a dark road that started when I realized I couldn't handle being around friends who were pregnant. I'm thirty-one years old, and all I've ever wanted to be was a wife and a mother. I'm neither. My jealousy toward the other women in my Bible study stirred up feelings of inadequacy. I kept wondering, *Why can't I find a mate? Is there no one out there who wants me for a wife?* The more I compared myself to others, the more I spiraled into self-doubt and ultimately depression.

Casey is a young, vibrant worship leader with an amazing voice, but she has recently wanted to withdraw from the worship team at her church. A new member of the team has excellent guitar skills, and the worship pastor seems to prefer her voice over Casey's, so Casey is not getting the opportunity to lead as much as she would like. She told me,

> I find myself comparing myself to Andrea, thinking thoughts like, *I can hit that note just as well* or *Her pitch isn't that great tonight and she's not annunciating clearly*. By tearing her down, I was trying to build up my own self-worth. When I found myself praying she wouldn't show up at practice, I knew something had to give. The breakthrough came for me one night as I was reading in a devotional book about how the Lord desires our worship, not a performance. That's when I knew I had to confess my envy and stop comparing myself to her.

Bailey has struggled with body image her entire life. After three kids, her body just isn't what it used to be. She wouldn't be caught dead in a bikini, but she resents women who look good in one.

As these stories show, performers are obsessed with measuring and comparing. We want to know if we measure up. But life was never meant to be a competition! Our significance and worth are anchored in God's grace alone. The more we find our significance in Christ's grace, the less we will battle envy. Conversely, the more we nurture and feed envy, the less we will experience God's grace.

In Matthew 20:1-16, Jesus told His followers a parable about our tendency to compare and become envious. Let's take a look at the story and then explore some practical steps we can take to slay the monster of envy.

The Parable of the Workers in the Field

Jesus began, "The kingdom of heaven is like a landowner who went out early in the morning to hire men to work in his vineyard." A typical workday in Palestine went from sunup to sundown. So at about six in the morning, the landowner went out to hire some men to work in his fields. The laborers agreed to work for the usual daily wage, which would have been about a denarius for one day's labor.[1] Everyone agreed to the terms. Boss and employees were both happy.

At nine o'clock, the landowner found other workers hanging around the marketplace, "doing nothing" (verse 3). The New Revised Standard Version says they were "standing idle." Hmmm. Not exactly the type of people you might look to employ. But the landowner offered each one a position. He didn't clarify how much each one was going to earn, only that it would be "right." Later, at about noon, the landowner again went out and invited more workers to his fields. He did the same at three o'clock and again at five o'clock, which meant this last group would work in the field for about an hour.

At sundown, all the workers gathered to receive their pay. The landowner began with those hired last and paid them a denarius. Then he paid the employees he had hired at three o'clock, and they also received a denarius. The rest of the workers were observing all this, and the tension began to rise. The guys who were hired first were most likely thinking, *Surely, we'll get paid more because we've been working here all day*. But as each worker moved forward to receive his wages, everyone received the same: a denarius.

Now the landowner had a riot on his hands. Imagine how the workers felt who were hired at the beginning of the day. They had slaved all day in the hot sun. The workers who had come at the end of the day had worked only one hour. Tempers started to flare and the murmur of grumblings grew until there was an uprising of, "We got ripped off. This isn't fair" (see verses 11-12).

The landowner calmly replied, "Friend, I am not being unfair to you. Didn't you agree to work for a denarius? Take your pay and go" (verses 13-14). Then he said, "Don't I have the right to do what I want with my own money? Or are you envious because I am generous?" (verse 15).

Obviously, the landowner could pay whatever he wished. After all, it was *his* money. So what was the real problem? The envy of the workers. They compared their wages with the wages of the latecomers and were dissatisfied.

God has the right to distribute gifts as He pleases. Any gift, whether an ability or a relationship or something else, is from Him. And God does not measure out His gifts equally. I don't understand why; I simply know it is true. He has the right, just like the landowner, to give what He desires.

GRACE GLIMPSE

Grace isn't fair. If I am going to find freedom from performing, I must stop comparing.

Serious Business

Webster defines *envy* as "the painful or resentful awareness of an advantage enjoyed by another joined with a desire to possess the same advantage."[2] In the New Testament, when the word *envy* is used, it means "the feeling of displeasure produced by witnessing or hearing of the advantage or prosperity of others."[3] For the performer, envy is the resentment felt when someone enjoys more approval or greater achievement.

Envy is wrong. It is the opposite of contentment, and as Christ followers, we are called to cultivate contentment (see 1 Timothy 6:6). Left unchecked, it damages our relationships, disrupts unity in churches, and devastates our spiritual walks. To help you understand just how destructive envy can be, I want to talk about women from Scripture.

Remember the story of Jacob and his two wives, Leah and Rachel (see Genesis 29–30)? Jacob worked for Laban, Leah and Rachel's father, with the understanding that after seven years he would marry Rachel, the younger daughter. Rachel was beautiful and Jacob loved her. When the seven years were up, Jacob married his bride. However, the morning after the wedding, he discovers that he had married Leah and not Rachel. (Leah likely had her face covered during the night.) He was ticked. Who could blame him? When Jacob confronted his father-in-law, he was told that if he worked another seven years, he could have Rachel as well. So Jacob ended up with both sisters. But life was not so happy at home. Jacob adored Rachel and put up with Leah.

This made Leah envy Rachel. After all, she had what Leah wanted: Jacob's love and attention. God felt sorry for Leah because she was so unloved, so he "opened her womb" (29:31) and she began having children. Each time she gave birth, she thought, *Now my husband will love me.* But Jacob's feelings for her didn't change, and as she watched the love and attention Jacob gave Rachel, Leah became more envious.

Even though Rachel was loved, she too felt envious. Leah had something that Rachel wanted: children. Women in biblical times measured their worth by their ability to bear children, and Rachel was "barren" (verse 31). One day she told Jacob, "Give me children, or I'll die" (30:1). Talk about hormonal! This was an irrational demand. Obviously, Jacob's body was not the problem, as Leah continued to get pregnant by him. When envy takes over, we fixate on the object we want and it becomes all we think or care about.

Leah's jealousy also pushed her to irrational thinking. Groping for love and a sense of purpose, she built her identity around her ability to have children. When menopause hit and she could not give birth, she gave her maidservant to Jacob. Her maid became pregnant with a son whom Leah named Asher. Asher means "happy." Leah thought to herself, "How happy I am! The women will call me happy" (verse 13).

Now, let me bring this home to those of you who are moms. Many moms build their identities and their emotional well-being around their kids. When their children don't live up to their expectations, they feel devastated. When a mom's emotional well-being revolves around her kids, she is in serious trouble because they are separate beings from her. They have the freedom to make their own choices and go their own way. Regardless of what our children do, our emotional well-being is to be centered on the truth that we are fully known, loved, forgiven, empowered, and pursued by God.

Ultimately, envy is serious business because it robs us of finding our significance in God's grace. When I compare myself or my life to others, a deficit develops in my soul. That deficit craves more, and soon God's grace doesn't feel like enough.

Keep in mind that every gift and ability we have been given is a measure of God's grace to us (see James 1:17). Each gift that comes from God's gracious, generous hand is to be enjoyed and received as a gift from Him for His glory. The gifts He gives are not to boost our egos. When God offers us His gifts and we look at the gifts of another and start whining, "I want more," it is as if we are accusing, "Your grace is not enough."

Envy shouts at God, "I won't be happy until . . ." When I believe this lie, I become fixated on the one thing I feel I cannot live without. This was Leah and Rachel's problem. The more we obsess about the "one thing," the less we believe how deeply God loves us. This is when Satan tempts us with the lie "If God really loved you, He would give you ____________________." Our joy is to be rooted in the immense love of God, not in His gifts.

Dear reader, God's grace *is* enough. He has given you all you need (see 2 Corinthians 12:9). Stop comparing.

It's Time to Change the Recipe

It occurs to me that we performers have all the ingredients for mixing up a batch of envy. Take our persistent question *Do I measure up?* and combine it with our desire for applause and tendency to compare ourselves with others. Stir in the fact that God distributes gifts in different measures, and mix it all together. *Voila!* We have the perfect recipe for envy and plummeting self-esteem. I think it's time we change the recipe, don't you?

So here's a new recipe for overcoming envy and finding our security in God's grace.

Ingredient #1: One Heaping Cup of Worship

Worship the Giver of the gifts, not the gifts themselves. God's gifts to us are an expression of His grace, but they are never to be worshipped. When we begin to place high value on those gifts, we are in danger of making them into idols.

Every gift and anointing comes as a result of God's empowering grace. It's up to God who gets what. To some He bestows extraordinary gifts; to others He gives average gifts; to still others He gives just small gifts. "We have different gifts according to the grace given us" (Romans 12:6), Paul said. "But by the grace of God I am what I am, and his grace to me was not without effect" (1 Corinthians 15:10). God doles out giftedness to each person as He decides best. When God gives gifts, it is for the edification of others. Your gifts are not to be the basis of your self-worth. (We're going to talk about this more in the next chapter, where we'll discuss giving up our obsession with perfection.)

When I find myself mixing the old recipe for envy, I stop and praise God for who He is and that He has gifted me according to His plan, not mine. Part of His grace is that He knows me completely. He knows exactly what I can handle and what I cannot. The more I worship and praise God rather than crave other gifts, the more He replaces my envy with a quiet assurance that He knows best. Whether big or small, every gift given to me comes from God and as such is perfect for me.

When I learned to worship the Giver of the gifts, His Spirit filled my heart with the deep reassurance that I am significant, not because of how well I perform but simply because God loves me. The longing for more "impressive" gifts has been quieted in me as my heart has been filled with the confidence that what I long for most I have in Jesus.

One of the ways I learned this was through the dangerous but wonderful journey of cancer. Before I had breast cancer, I considered myself to be a person of great energy, but since cancer and all subsequent surgeries, my energy levels are not what they used to be. At times, I have become frustrated and begged God for more energy. In those moments, God has reminded me that any energy I have is a gift from Him and that His energy is made perfect in my lack of energy. He loves me whether I have a lot of energy or none. Some of the most intimate experiences I've had with Him have been when I'm exhausted.

While in prison for his faith, John Bunyan wrote *Grace Abounding to the Chief of Sinners*. In this autobiographical sketch of his conversion and call to ministry, Bunyan penned these words: "Gifts are desirable, but great grace and small gifts are better than great gifts and no grace."[4] Worship Jesus Christ, who is the Giver of the gifts; don't worship the gifts.

Ingredient #2: One Half Cup of Positive and True Self-Talk

Whenever I am tempted to measure how I compare with others, I remind myself of the truth that "I am fearfully and wonderfully made" (Psalm 139:14). God designed me with intention, and the more I tell myself this truth, the more it makes its way down into my heart.

Try it this week and see if it helps. Whenever you are ready to compare yourself to someone, catch yourself and begin rehearsing the truth that you are fearfully and wonderfully made. God designed and created you uniquely. There is no one like you. You have a specific design, story, and calling. You don't have to be the best at everything. There will always be others who are better than you at something or who enjoy more success than you. That doesn't change your value one iota.

Ingredient # 3: More Than a Pinch of Gratitude

The apostle Paul wrote, "Do not be anxious about anything, but in everything, by prayer and petition, with thanksgiving, present your requests to God. And the peace of God, which transcends all understanding, will guard your hearts and your minds in Christ" (Philippians 4:6-7). The more I give thanks for the gifts God gives me, the more He fills my life with joy. The more I give thanks for my husband's love and affirmation, the less likely I am to crave the attention other women might get from their husbands. My ravenous appetite for affirmation is quieted as I give thanks. We are going to come back to this idea of gratitude in chapter 11, but before we move on, I want to show you a practical step for cultivating gratitude when you struggle with envy.

Courtney cultivates an attitude of gratitude by keeping a daily log of things she is thankful for. At the front of her journal, she has this quote by Thomas Merton: "Nurturing gratitude re-creates the goodness of God within us, helping us to 'recognize' the Love of God in everything he has given us—and he has given us everything."[5] Some days are discouraging for this new mom who longs to make a difference for God. As Courtney has been faithful at keeping a thankful list, she has seen a huge change in her attitude. She envies far less because she is far more content. Here is a sampling of the kinds of things she gives thanks for every day:

- The chance to talk to a friend and encourage her
- Her boys napping until four in the afternoon
- The work God is doing in her life to free her from fear
- The ability to trust God more today than the day before
- Warmer temperatures
- Her husband's love
- The delight of her one-year-old daughter's laugh

Did you notice that the things on Courtney's list were simple, everyday things? That's just the point of giving thanks regularly. We can't just wait to give God thanks for the miraculous; we must give Him thanks for the little moments of life. The more we give Him thanks, the less that envy will bother us and the more we will experience contentment.

William Law wrote, "If I could tell you the shortest, surest way to all happiness and all perfection, it would be to make a rule for yourself to thank and praise God for everything that happens to you. For it is certain that whatever seeming calamity may happen to you, if you thank and praise God for it, you turn it into a blessing."[6] I find these words profound and true. If we praise and thank God in every situation, He is honored and the Holy Spirit quickens our hearts with joy. I am not talking about being fake here. Authentically share your hurts, disappointments, frustrations, and grief with God, but then choose to praise Him and give Him thanks above the pain and sorrow. Then your gratitude becomes a sacrifice of praise (see Psalm 50:23).

Ingredient #4: A Tablespoon of Rejoicing When Others Rejoice

I can almost guarantee you won't feel like rejoicing when others receive a larger bonus than you, when God blesses a friend with a baby and you are infertile, or when your friend's child receives honors in school and your child needs special help. But I believe if you consistently choose to rejoice with others, it gets easier to do, even for hard things. We choose with our minds and trust that our feelings will follow.

The apostle Paul wrote that we are to "rejoice with those who rejoice; mourn with those who mourn" (Romans 12:15). Sometimes mourning is easier. But as we intentionally choose to rejoice with those who are experiencing more success or affirmation than we are, God is glorified in our lives. Isn't that what it's all about?

Ingredient #5: A Generous Portion of the Holy Spirit

I have found that unless I continually ask the Holy Spirit to change me, it's easy to fall back into old patterns. Ultimately, He is the greatest change agent we have. He is like the baking soda in a recipe that causes the cake or cookies to rise. He is more than willing to change us as we cooperate with Him. Jesus said that the reason He would leave His Spirit is so we would not have to be responsible for our own spiritual transformation. He promised that the Holy Spirit would be our teacher and our guide in our journey to be more like Jesus (see John 14:25-26).

Self-Examination and Confession

Most of us will continue to battle envy until we die, so my advice is simple: Ask the Holy Spirit to reveal to you any envious thoughts you have. As soon as you are aware of envy in your life, confess it to the Lord, ask Him to forgive you, and redirect your thoughts. The longer we focus on the envy, the more we become entangled in it. So don't engage in morbid speculation. Don't beat yourself up. Simply confess, thank God that you're forgiven, and move on!

When we are convinced that we are fully known, love, forgiven, empowered, and pursued by God, it is easier to view ourselves realistically—to see our faults and our weaknesses—because our significance is found in His grace. When someone else has stronger gifts or abilities than we do, we can rest in the assurance that God is working in our lives. We don't have to be a star to be valuable. We are enough, just as we are.

Message from the Grace Giver

> My child, stop comparing yourself to others. You don't have to be the best at anything in order to be valuable. I love you just the way I created you. Every ability you possess is a gift from Me (see James 1:17). I'm proud of the gifts I have given you. Instead of comparing them to the gifts of others, come to Me with thanksgiving for what I have given you (see Psalm 136:1). Surrender your envy to Me, moment by moment. As you do, I will gradually replace your envy with a spirit of thankfulness, and you will grow more confident in My grace.

Praying Scripture to Internalize Grace

Thank You, Almighty One, that You have designed me according to Your purpose and for the pleasure of Your will. How I praise You that before You even formed me in my mother's womb, You knew me and set me apart for Your purposes (see Jeremiah 1:5). How I praise You that You take delight in me and crown me with salvation (see Psalm 149:4). I praise You because I am fearfully and wonderfully made (see Psalm 139:14).

Lord, my feet have slipped from time to time as I have envied those who are more prosperous and successful than I am (see Psalm 73:3). You tell me not be envious but to delight in You and that You will give me the desires of my heart (see Psalm 37:1,4). I confess that sometimes it feels as though You are overlooking my desires and granting the desires of others. At those times, jealousy burns in my heart. Your Word warns me that envy is destructive to my well-being (see Proverbs 14:30) and that if I truly love someone, I will not envy him or her (see 1 Corinthians 13:4). Teach me not to compare myself to others but to allow Your Holy Spirit to love them through me.

I know that envy does not help me experience Your grace. Holy One, forgive me and create in me a pure heart so that I can fully experience Your grace. Renew a steadfast spirit within me (see Psalm 51:10). Your Word promises that if I confess my sins, You are faithful and just and will forgive my sins and purify me from all unrighteousness (see 1 John 1:9). I can rest in the forgiveness You offer today.

Lord, teach me to trust Your love. Today I choose to meditate on Your love rather than on the success of others (see Psalm 48:9). I will be still before You and wait patiently for You (see Psalm 37:7). Remind me throughout this day to wait for You and to keep Your ways. Thank You that at the right moment You will exalt me to inherit Your blessings (see Psalm 37:34).

My hope is in You (see Psalm 39:7).

A Daily Dose of Grace

Day 1

1. Memorize and meditate on 1 Corinthians 1:30-31 as written here or in another translation:

   > It is because of him that you are in Christ Jesus, who has become for us wisdom from God—that is, our righteousness, holiness and redemption. Therefore, as it is written: "Let him who boasts boast in the Lord."

2. According to 1 Corinthians 1:30-31, what is the only valid cause for boasting?

Day 2

1. Read Matthew 20:1-16. Imagine that you are one of the first workers hired. Describe how you feel when the landowner pays everyone the same wage.

2. The landowner responds to the workers, "Or are you envious because I am generous?" (Matthew 20:15). Think about the word *generous*. God's grace is generous, but sometimes it feels as though He is more generous to some than to others. Do you think God plays favorites? Why, or why not?

3. Write your own definition for *envy.*

Day 3

1. Read 1 Corinthians 3:1-4. Describe the problem in the church at Corinth. Why do you think Paul describes envy as an immature emotion?

2. Read James 3:16 and Galatians 5:15. How can envy destroy relationships?

3. Read Galatians 5:16-26. What does Paul mean by the words "Live by the Spirit"? How can living by the Spirit help a person overcome envy?

Day 4

1. Read 1 Samuel 18:1-11 and 19:1-2 and then answer the following questions:

   a. Why did Saul feel envious of David?

   b. How did Saul's jealousy affect his ability to think clearly?

   c. What lessons are there in these verses for the person who struggles with envy?

   d. What did God say to you personally through these verses?

Day 5

1. In what areas of life do you struggle with envy?

2. Read Colossians 3:17. How might giving thanks help you overcome envy?

3. Read James 1:17. What does it look like for you to worship the Giver of the gifts more than the gifts themselves?

Day 6

1. Review 1 Corinthians 1:30-31.

2. Spend some quiet moments with the Lord. Ask Him to reveal to you any people you feel envious toward. In the space provided, write those people's names down. Then pray a prayer of confession, asking God to cleanse you from envy. Ask God to bless each of the individuals you listed.

CHAPTER 7

LET GO OF BEING PERFECT

Do not dwell upon your inner failings. . . . Just do this: Bring your soul to the Great Physician—exactly as you are, even and especially at your worst moment. . . . For it is in such moments that you will most readily sense His healing presence.

TERESA OF AVILA

When I think of the old hymn "Our Best," I feel sick to my stomach. If you love that old hymn, I don't mean to offend you. It's just that I remember the scene so well.

My father had decided to have us sing at a Bible conference where he was the guest speaker. I remember how excited I was that this was our big debut. Who knew? Maybe we would be invited to sing at other venues or even on the radio someday! We had practiced diligently, singing, "Hear ye the Master's call, 'Give me thy best.'" My older sister was going to sing alto, and my younger sister and I were going to carry the soprano.

The night of our performance, my sisters and I wore matching pink dresses. Halfway into the first verse, we started giggling. We tried to stifle our laughter, but it just wasn't working. The audience grew uncomfortable, wondering what would happen next. The pianist continued, hoping we would regain our composure. It didn't happen. Clutching our tummies, we laughed so hard we nearly wet our pants. Unable to stop, we exited the stage, and the pianist finished the song without us.

No one was happy with us that night. Later, in the dark, I apologized to God. He had asked us for our best, and giggling off the stage was definitely not "our best." I felt so disappointed in myself.

That little episode doesn't stand alone. Growing up, I felt a lot of pressure to bring God my best, but my best felt difficult to measure. How could I know for sure if I had brought God my best? I couldn't, so I set higher goals for myself: read my Bible more, keep a better prayer list, get better grades in school, be kinder to my siblings, on and on it went. When my performance wasn't perfect, I felt like a failure. After all, to be a Christian meant to be like Christ. He was perfect, and I could never quite get there. With failure, my perfectionism only got worse. I would rededicate, recommit, and restate my intentions to try harder to be like Jesus. I lived with constant fear that God felt disappointed in me.

This fear followed me into adulthood, as did my perfectionism. When I married and had my own home, I never felt satisfied with my abilities to organize or my cooking. Pie crusts, cookies, and cakes all had to measure up to Martha Stewart or I felt disappointed. With all the entertaining we did in ministry, I had plenty of opportunity to try, but I always thought I could have done better. I longed for my husband to observe how perfect I was, and so when my efforts went unnoticed, I struggled inwardly with anger toward him. I tried in every way to be the Proverbs 31 woman, and after a while I resented her. (If you are unfamiliar with the passage, check it out and you'll understand my angst.) As a pastor's wife, I struggled with a sort of "Superwoman complex," trying to be everything I thought a pastor's wife should be. I taught Sunday school and Bible studies, entertained frequently, and directed Daily Vacation Bible School during the summer.

When I became a mother, my perfectionism skyrocketed. I had unwritten rules for myself: Never speak a sharp word to my children, make sure they don't get dirty (difficult because at the time my oldest was a baby and we were living in Sudan, East Africa, where the dirt and dust continually blew in our windows!), read them stories, play educational games with them every day, spend time praying with them every day, and pray over them every night. I wanted to enjoy every minute of being a mom, but my rules left me uptight and worried about whether I was parenting the "right" way.

Although perfectionism created much anxiety for me, it also served me well. Others admired my efforts and congratulated me on a job well done. If I did something perfectly or close to it, I avoided criticism. My perfectionism helped me keep my world organized and in control, at least externally. It helped me take my roles as wife, mother, and ministry leader seriously and propelled me to be as intentional as possible about improving in every one of those areas.

But overall my perfectionism did me more harm than good. It left me exhausted from trying so hard and anxious that I could do better. At night I would reflect back on the day and think, *I will do better tomorrow.* At times, I projected my perfectionism onto others, and they felt the pressure of my unrealistic expectations. Other times, I held myself back because I wasn't sure I could do something perfectly. Sometimes my perfectionism paralyzed me because I got stuck obsessing about the "right" decision and was unable to make any decision. The question that most haunted me was this: *When I get to heaven, will I hear, "Well done, good and faithful servant"?* (Matthew 25:21).

Jesus told a story that includes those words. Performers need to understand that God is not calling us to be perfect; instead, He is calling us to be faithful.

The Parable of the Talents

In Matthew 25, Jesus tells a story about a man who was going on a long journey and left his servants in charge of some of his assets. He told them to wisely invest and to multiply his money while he was gone.

"To one he gave five talents of money, to another two talents, and to another one talent, each according to his ability" (verse 15). A talent was a sum of money; some say it was worth more than a thousand dollars in today's economy.[1] The master in this story knew his servants well and distributed the money accordingly. When he returned, he called the three servants and wanted a report. The first reported that he took the five talents and put them to work right away. He doubled the master's money. The master was overjoyed and slapped the fellow on the back, saying, "Well done, good and faithful servant!" and promised him more responsibility.

The second servant also invested wisely and reported that he had doubled the master's money. The master excitedly cheered, "Well done, good and faithful servant!" and promised this servant more responsibility.

The last servant had not invested the money well. He accused the master of being unreasonable and demanding and explained that he had felt afraid and so had dug a hole in the ground and hid the money there. The master was furious. No kudos for this servant. Instead, the master called him lazy and wicked.

How are we, especially performers, to interpret this story? How do we get that "Well done" from God? As I have thought about this question and studied this passage, the word that jumped off the page at me is the word *faithful.* I believe that this is a story about faithfulness, not perfection.

GRACE GLIMPSE

God values faithfulness, not perfection.

The master did not compliment the servants on a job done perfectly or even for working hard. He did not say, "Well done—you've been successful!" Instead, the focus of His delight was their faithfulness.

HOW DO YOU MEASURE FAITHFULNESS?

The word *faithful* appears over and over again in the New Testament. The apostle Paul wrote, "It is required that those who have been given a trust must prove faithful" (1 Corinthians 4:2). In his letter to the church at Colosse, Paul describes Epaphras, Tychicus, and Onesimus as being faithful servants (see Colossians 1:7; 3:7,9). While we don't know much about those three men, we know none of them was perfect.

The writer of Hebrews describes Moses as "faithful as a servant" (3:5). He was absolutely *not* perfect. He murdered someone (see Exodus 2:12), argued with God about his assigned task (see 3:11; 4:1-14), and became so angry at the Israelites that he threw down the tablets with the Ten Commandments, smashing them to bits (see 32:19). In the end, he was not allowed to see the Promised Land because he didn't trust God enough (see verse 51). Despite his flaws and sins, God calls Moses faithful. What does He mean by this?

The idea behind the Greek word for faithful means "to be trusted, reliable."[2] In the parable, the servants were supposed to invest the talents for their master. This is why he was so displeased with the servant to which he gave only one talent. This servant was not reliable. He did not do as he was told.

What does it look like for a performer to be "trusted and reliable"—faithful—in God's eyes? Here are some principles I have found helpful in my journey toward faithfulness rather than perfection.

Faithfulness begins with the awareness that every gift and ability comes from God. The talent in the parable represents any gift given to us by the Lord, and it is to be used for His glory. The servants were not to draw their significance from the money given to them, nor were they to view the money as their own; they were to view it as something over which they were responsible until the master returned. Similarly, any gift given to us by God belongs to God and is to be for God's glory alone. When perfectionism enters the picture, it becomes about our glory and not His.

I have to remind myself of this frequently. The goal in using my gifts is not to find greater significance (I am already as significant as I will ever be to God) but to make God look bigger in my life. God doesn't call me to be famous; He calls me to be faithful. No matter what God calls me to do, I can offer that for His glory.

In addition, I am not supposed to develop my gifts for the sake of perfection but for God's glory. If the goal is perfection, I will freak out and may end up burying my talent for fear that what I offer is not good enough, just like the last servant.

Faithfulness calls us to continue, even when we are struggling with self-doubt. Self-doubt is an area where Satan continually tries to torment me. When I feel as though I am failing or fear that I am going to fail, I become paralyzed and can't move ahead. I am learning to redefine failure as "an opportunity for growth." When tasks or assignments don't turn out as well as I might like, instead of beating myself up, I ask the Lord to use the experience for growth in my life.

I did this recently while I was working on a writing project. Words weren't coming and I felt like quitting. Instead, I decided to take a break and spent some time reading my Bible. Some verses in Hebrews pierced my insecure heart: "Do not throw away your confidence; it will be richly rewarded. You need to persevere so that when you have done the will of God, you will receive what he has promised" (10:35-36). It was as if the Holy Spirit was whispering, "Becky, chill. Persevere and remain faithful. This is My will for you. Hang in there and keep working. Your effort will pay off. I've called you to do this. Hang in there with Me during the process. I am pleased with you; I don't require perfection. Don't throw away your confidence. Instead, lean into Me." What I have discovered is that the growth process in my life is just as important as the final product.

Faithfulness calls us to work for God, not the applause of others. This is what the apostle Paul meant when he wrote, "Whatever you do, work at it with all your heart, as working for the Lord, not for men" (Colossians 3:23).

Paul's words can be confusing, especially the phrase "Work at it with all your heart." You've probably heard that used many times by well-meaning Sunday school teachers. God does honor hard work, but that's not the point of this verse. Paul was addressing a specific problem in the church. He was writing in a time when wealthy Christians owned slaves, many of whom were coming to Christ. Some of the believers who read Paul's letter were slaves, and they had little opportunity to get out of slavery and find freedom. It would have been easy for them to become hopeless and resent their masters. In this verse, Paul was instructing the slaves to put themselves into their work and view every task as an opportunity to serve the Lord.[3] He assured them that their work had value in God's eyes and that He was pleased with them.

Paul did not intend this verse to be used to throw us on a guilt trip and into a sense of panic, wondering if we are working hard enough and performing well enough to please God; this verse is a call to a good work ethic. This means such things as arriving to work on time, not enjoying social networking when you are being paid by your company to do specific tasks, and maintaining a joyful spirit.

Faithfulness has nothing to do with wanting to be "the best." The desire to be the best is often rooted in one's desire to look good rather than make God look good.

Pride is Satan's number one tool to derail grace in your life. Beth Moore has wisely written, "The challenge to overcome pride may be the only common denominator on every one of our spiritual 'to-do' lists."[4] Satan tempts all of us in the area of pride, but it is my conviction that performers are the most prone. We can fool ourselves into believing that we don't struggle with pride—that we just want to do our best for God. Don't be fooled. Pride is lurking behind the mask of every performer. Beware and be wise. Take responsibility. When you feel yourself being pulled into perfectionism, ask God to show you any areas of your life where pride has crept in, and then humble yourself and ask Him to cleanse you. Proverbs warns that when pride comes, then comes disgrace, but with humility comes wisdom (see 11:2).

My fellow performers, let's ask God for the courage to face pride in ourselves. Unless we faithfully invite Him to remove it from us, we will not be able to experience fully the richness of His grace. We experience immeasurable freedom as we learn to ask Him to do the work through us.

Faithfulness involves asking God to live His life through me. Because I vacillate between self-doubt and pride, I have learned to continually, sometimes minute by minute, pray, *Lord, live Your life through me.* This simple prayer relieves me of the pressure to be perfect. Paul wrote, "We have this treasure in jars of clay to show that this all-surpassing power is from God and not from us" (2 Corinthians 4:7). We're not supposed to be a perfect clay pot. We're more effective broken! This realization has brought me great freedom. As long as I am broken, God's power is seen more clearly in my life. Someday I long to hear the words "Well done, Becky. Great job of being broken. Thanks for your faithfulness in letting Me live My life through you."

A Picture of Faithfulness

As we bring this chapter to a close, I want to tell you about "Grandpa Ed," as we affectionately call him. When I think of faithfulness, he is the perfect picture. As he and his wife, Lou, aged, she was diagnosed with Parkinson's disease. As Lou's disease progressed, Grandpa Ed faithfully took care of her, making sure she took her medicine, keeping her on an exercise schedule, cooking the meals, cleaning the house, and taking her to her doctor appointments. I never heard him complain. Faithfully and lovingly, he took care of his bride. But despite Grandpa

Ed's efforts, Lou eventually had to be admitted to a nursing home. Grandpa Ed could have plummeted into a depression, understandably so. Instead, he goes to the nursing home every day, but he even goes beyond that!

One Sunday he attended a small service for the nursing home residents. In the middle of the priest's homily, Grandpa Ed became somewhat agitated and raised his hand and asked if he could share a word. The priest agreed, so Grandpa Ed stood to his feet and gave testimony to Christ's grace, sharing how Jesus had changed his life. The priest was so impressed that he asked Grandpa Ed if he would be willing to lead a Bible study and take over the Sunday services. Grandpa Ed has never been to Bible college nor seminary so he felt ill-quipped. He knew he couldn't teach the Word perfectly or eloquently, but he decided he would try leading the Bible study. So at age eighty-seven, Grandpa Ed has taken on a new challenge. He is faithfully teaching a Bible study in the nursing home. Every week, residents are hearing about the grace of Jesus Christ and how they can receive that grace.

Grandpa Ed has become a living example of faithfulness to me. He loves and visits his dear wife every day, though she can hardly respond. And now he is regularly teaching a Bible study, sharing the message of God's grace with residents who at times are indifferent or even cranky.

Is Grandpa Ed perfect? No. Is he a big success by the world's standards? No. But is he faithful? You bet! When he steps into heaven for the first time, I imagine Jesus will be the first of many to say, "Well done, Ed. I'm so proud of you!"

Message from the Grace Giver

> My child, learn to relax and enjoy My presence more. You feel so worried about pleasing Me. I want you to learn to enjoy doing nothing except being with Me. The more you faithfully focus on My presence, the less you will worry about

> succeeding. Take the gifts I have given you and use them for My glory. They may feel little from your perspective, but not from Mine. You don't have to be the best in order to hear "Well done" from Me. In fact, you might be surprised at who I reward for faithfulness in heaven. It might not be those who outwardly accomplished the most. It might be the poor, the bruised, and the broken. Simply ask Me each morning, "Lord, what would You have me do today?" Whatever I call you to, I will faithfully do through you (see 1 Thessalonians 5:24).

Praying Scripture to Internalize Grace

Lord, how I thank You that You don't call me to be perfect but to be faithful. Like the apostle Paul, I have not obtained perfection but press on faithfully to take hold of that for which Christ Jesus took hold of me (see Philippians 3:11). I praise You that You are always faithful in my life, even when I am not faithful (see 1 Corinthians 1:9; 2 Timothy 2:13). You understand that I am a broken clay pot. Because of my insufficiencies, others can see that what's happening in my life has nothing to do with my abilities but with Your all-surpassing power (see 2 Corinthians 4:7). Thank You that Your Holy Spirit is at work within me, changing me moment by moment as I yield to Him (see 1 Thessalonians 5:23). How I praise You that I don't have to change myself. You have promised to transform me by Your faithfulness (see verse 24).

Thank You that though I am imperfect and often don't even know how to pray, the Holy Spirit prays for me and through me (see Romans 8:26). Your Word tells me that You take my mistakes and turn them around for my good (see verse 28). You lead me in triumphal procession, and through me You spread the fragrance of the knowledge of God (see 2 Corinthians 2:14).

I praise You that You will enable me to finish the race faithfully as I depend on You (see 2 Timothy 4:7). Like the apostle Paul, my goal is to finish well and complete the tasks You have called me to do. Thank You that part of that task is to share Your message of grace (see Acts 2:24). I praise You that You are able to make all grace abound to me so that in all things, at all times, having all that I need, I will abound in every good work (see 2 Corinthians 9:8). Help me not to become weary in doing good, because You have promised that if I remain faithful and persevere, I will reap the benefits of my work (see Galatians 6:9). Lord, I want to remain faithful to You, not just for a reward but out of a heart of gratitude for the continual grace You have shown me.

A DAILY DOSE OF GRACE

Day 1

1. Memorize and meditate on Philippians 3:12 as written here or in another translation:

   > Not that I have already obtained all this, or have already been made perfect, but I press on to take hold of that for which Christ Jesus took hold of me.

2. In what areas of your life have you struggled with perfectionism? How has that impacted your relationship with Christ?

3. Read Philippians 3:12 again. What does it mean to you to "press on"?

Day 2

1. Read the story of the talents (see Matthew 25:1-13). Why do you think the servant hid the one talent he had received?

2. Read 1 Timothy 6:11. What does this verse teach about the nature of faithfulness?

3. Write your own definition for *faithfulness*.

Day 3

1. Read Philippians 3:12-14. What does it look like in your life to "strain toward"? Do you think Paul is implying that we are to strive for perfection? Why, or why not?

2. Look at some different aspects of your life—marriage, parenting, job, service to the church, someone you are witnessing to—and then write a sentence about what it looks like in that area of your life to be faithful and strain toward.

3. Read Hebrews 12:1-2. What does it look like for a person to run with endurance? What types of things might hinder our running with faithfulness?

Day 4

1. Read Titus 2:1-6. What can we learn about faithfulness from these verses? Is there one idea that stands out to you from this passage? If so, write your thoughts. What would it look like for you to put that principle into practice?

2. Think of an older woman you know who is a model of the principles found in Titus 2:1-6. What qualities do you see in her that exemplify faithfulness? List those qualities here.

Day 5

1. How would you define success? How do you measure your own success?

2. Read 1 Peter 4:10. According to this verse, how can we measure faithfulness?

3. Read 2 Timothy 2:2. Paul instructed Timothy to be strong and to entrust the message of the gospel to men who were reliable. How would you describe someone who is reliable? If Timothy were the pastor in your church, would he trust you with a position of leadership? Why, or why not?

Day 6

1. Review Philippians 3:12.

2. What have you learned this week about living a faithful life?

3. Read 1 Thessalonians 5:24. What is your part in living a faithful life, and what is God's part in empowering you to live a faithful life?

4. Describe how a new principle you learned from this chapter might help you be faithful in a particularly difficult area of your life.

CHAPTER 8

Discover Your True Belovedness

God is indeed a wonderful Father who longs to pour out His mercy upon us and whose majesty is so great that He can transform us from deep within.

Teresa of Avila

Many of us believe that our belovedness is rooted in how well we perform. These feelings often originate in childhood, with parents who offered conditional love and acceptance. Certainly this was the case for Lisa and Vicki.

Lisa grew up in a home where achievement and appearance were important. Her father, an emotionally distant college professor, expected his children to excel in school. This wasn't a problem for her siblings, but Lisa, who has dyslexia, struggled with school. Her grades never measured up to her father's expectations. She remembers the humiliation she felt when she had to line up with her siblings to show him her report card. While her sisters and brothers presented report cards filled with A's and B's, Lisa's report card held C's and D's. Her father would praise her siblings and then angrily accuse Lisa of being lazy. Punishment and more humiliation inevitably followed.

Lisa's mother was obsessed with weight and also set impossible standards for her children. Lisa remembers being marched into the doctor's office, asked to step on the scale, and then hearing her mother tell the doctor she wanted her daughter to go on a diet.

When she turned eighteen, Lisa gave up trying to please her parents and ran away from home to marry the man of her dreams. All her emotional baggage followed her into that marriage, and years later, Lisa still struggles with an inner compulsion to perform well so that others will accept her.

Vicki grew up with a bipolar mother and an emotionally distant father. Her mother's mood swings ruled the family. One tiny mistake could catapult her mom into fits of anger, so Vicki tried hard to never make a mistake. Her father, buried under the load of trying to stay on top of household chores, had little time for Vicki, and she grew up with an enormous need for affirmation and approval. In some part of her mind, Vicki felt sure that God must be similar to her father.

Like Lisa and Vicki, many women who struggle with performance issues grew up feeling they could never measure up to the standards their parents set at home. Consequently, they have adopted the belief that they must perform well to earn God's love.

At one point in His earthly ministry, Jesus asked, "Which of you, if his son asks for bread, will give him a stone? Or if he asks for a fish, will give him a snake?" (Matthew 7:9-10). Even though what Jesus suggests here is preposterous, this is how some of us were treated by our parents. Instead of nurturing us, they gave us the stone of emotional coldness. Instead of giving us gifts that would feed and nourish our souls, they gave us biting criticism, or even abuse, which poisoned our spirits. This caused us to be tied to the message "I can never be good enough, or do enough, to be loved by you." Sadly, this belief drives us even as adults, causing us to try as hard as we can to earn love.

We may believe in some cognitive way that God loves us, because after all, He's God and He's supposed to love us, but we still have difficulty *feeling* loved by Him. Why would God love us?

If you struggle with feeling loved by God, then this chapter is for you! Girlfriend, God doesn't just want you to know cognitively that He loves you; He wants you to *feel* His love. He wants you to find the deep security that comes from knowing that He sees you as His beloved child and His feelings for you will never change, no matter how well or how badly you perform. He is categorically in love with you!

Jesus knew that if we were going to internalize this amazing love, He would have to paint a different portrait of God than the picture we have in our heads of our earthly parents. This is exactly what He did in the story about the lost son (see Luke 15:11-32).

My prayer for you, dear reader, is that you will get a glimpse of how deeply Abba Father loves you and that by the end of the chapter, you will be dancing in the security of knowing you are His beloved daughter.

THE PARABLE OF THE LOST SON

Here's a quick summary of the story Jesus told in Luke 15:11-32. A father had two sons. One day the younger son asked the father for his inheritance, and the father gave him his portion. The son took his inheritance, moved far away from his father's rules and restrictions, and spent all his money on partying, women, and lavish living. Shortly after all his money was gone, a famine hit the country in which he was living and the son fell on hard times and got a job feeding pigs so he could eat. He then came to his senses and decided to go back home and ask his father to hire him. But when he returned home, he received a different homecoming than what he expected.

That's the storyline. Now let's look a bit closer at what is going on between the lines so that we can gain a deeper understanding of what's on Jesus' mind. Then we'll draw some implications for those of us struggling to feel God's love.

The younger son's request would have rocked the family system.

Kenneth E. Bailey, a professor and lecturer in Middle Eastern New Testament studies, wrote, "It was unthinkable for any son to request his portion of the family wealth while his father was still alive. Every Middle Eastern peasant understands this instinctively."[1] The son may not have broken the law by asking his father for his inheritance early, but his request broke his father's heart. Why? Because such a request would mean that the son wished his father were already dead.

Such an unorthodox request would also hurt the family clan. Each family supported the economy of the entire village, and for a son to suddenly pull out his portion of the inheritance meant the entire village would take a financial hit. So when the younger son took his inheritance and left home, he was cut off from the entire village because he had shamed no only his father but also his village. This son lost his rights in his immediate family and also in the family clan.

If ever a kid were a failure, this kid was it! He lost all of his dad's hard-earned money and had nothing to show for it. He was in such desperate straits that he took the lowest of low jobs, getting paid less than minimum wage. No wonder he plummeted into despair. "When he came to his senses, he said, 'How many of my father's hired men have food to spare, and here I am starving to death! I will set out and go back to my father and say to him: Father, I have sinned against heaven and against you. I am no longer worthy to be called your son; make me like one of your hired men'" (verses 17-19).

I used to believe that this was the point of repentance in the younger son's life, but now I believe differently. The language is similar to how Pharaoh confessed to Moses: "I have sinned against the Lord your God and against you" (Exodus 10:16). Pharaoh's confession was insincere and more an attempt to manipulate Moses into retracting the plague. The way the son's confession is worded, it sounds like he planned to go home, apologize to soften his father's heart, and offer to work for his father so that he could eat.[2] He was trying to earn his dad's favor. He was not offering to go home as a son but as a servant. He hoped to redeem himself.

At this point in the story, there was an astonishing turn of events. The father saw the son approaching the outskirts of the village. He knew what would happen when his son tried to reenter the village. The law dictated that if a "Jewish boy lost the family inheritance among Gentiles and dared to return home, the community would break a large pot in front of him and cry out 'so-in-so is cut off from his people.' The ceremony was called the *Kezazah* (literally 'the cutting off')."[3] The father knew that if his son returned home, gangs of teenage boys would follow him through the village, mocking him and shouting insults.

He couldn't bear this thought, so he ran toward his son to get to him before the villagers reached him. The Greek word here for *run*[4] speaks of racing. He gathered the front edges of his robe, exposing his legs, so that he could run to his son. It would have been considered an extremely shameful posture for a Jewish father, as head of the family clan, to expose his legs like this. In doing so, the father took on the shame that belonged to his son and saved him from the punishment he deserved. The whole village would have seen the grace that the father offered to his son.

What an amazing picture of both the Incarnation and the Atonement! The father's actions made reconciliation possible. The son said, "Father, I have sinned against . . . you. I am no longer worthy to be called your son" (Luke 15:21). Here was the son's genuine repentance. He realized what it cost his father to run to him and that it was an act of reconciliation. Overwhelmed with his father's gracious love, the son didn't follow through with his intention of offering to work for his father. He was ready to receive his father's grace. He repented and accepted the offer of reconciliation.

Once the son was home and all was reconciled, the father threw a party. He placed on his son his most elegant robe and his signet ring, all signs of his love and approval. There was no lecturing, rebuking, or scolding. All was well for this younger son who messed up and failed so badly.

Meanwhile, the older brother had been working hard in the fields. He was the obedient son, the responsible one, the rule follower. He had been trying so hard for so long to be good enough. When he heard the sounds of the party and the singing and dancing, he called a servant over and inquired about the noise coming from the house. He was shocked and ticked to learn that his father had thrown a party for his rebellious little brother. After all, he'd been the obedient son, and their father had never given a party for him! Filled with rage, he refused to go in to the celebration. Once again, the father's response to his son's disrespectful behavior is astonishing. Instead of disowning the older son for disrespecting him, the father left his guests and went to the older son and pled with him (see verse 28). The father demonstrated no anger here, only grace.

I believe that Jesus told this story to give us not only a clearer picture of grace but also a new picture of God as our Father. He left the glory of heaven to run toward us in grace. God never gives up on us, even when we reject His love. He consistently offers grace to both the sinner and the righteous. He initiates and makes reconciliation possible. It's such a different kind of love than what many of us grew up with, it takes my breath away. Abba never stops pursuing us, no matter if we mess up or not.

GRACE GLIMPSE

I am God's beloved daughter, no matter how well I perform.

We live in a world that applauds good behavior and punishes wrong behavior. The culture in which we live says, "I will love you if you perform well enough." God says, "I love you completely, no matter how well you perform." When you think about it, that's pretty crazy!

A Portrait of God's Heart

Let's sum up what this parable teaches us about God's heart:

God is brokenhearted when we reject His love. We reject God's love when we strive harder to earn His approval, when we run after other loves to fill the ache in our hearts that only God can fill, and when we punish ourselves rather than accept the atonement that Christ alone can accomplish. Our rejection of God's love breaks His heart. We see this throughout Scripture. The prophet Isaiah captures the sorrow God feels when His love is rejected: "Let me weep bitterly. Do not try to console me over the destruction of my people" (Isaiah 22:4). When Jesus entered Jerusalem, riding on a colt, He saw the city and began to weep, expressing again the sorrow of rejected love. Luke wrote, "As he approached Jerusalem and saw the city, he wept over it and said, 'If you, even you, had only known on this day what would bring you peace'" (Luke 19:41-42). What a picture of God's longing for us to receive and embrace His love.

God is full of compassion toward us when we mess up. You may have grown up with parents who were not compassionate toward you when you did not perform up to their standards. Abba Father is different. In the story, when the father saw his son, he was filled with "compassion" (Luke 15:20). "The Greek word for 'have compassion' has as its root 'innards.'"[5] Easterners saw the intestines as the center of the emotions, so whenever a family member was hurt or rejected, another villager would say, "You are cutting up my intestines." The phrase gives a picture of the sickening feeling we get in our stomach when we hear something tragic. The father in the story felt what his son was feeling, and this caused him to run to him in order to save him from being punished and taunted. Similarly, God, moved with compassion, sent Jesus to reach us and take our punishment so that we would not have to receive the punishment due us. Our heavenly Father continually runs toward us, inviting us home to receive and enjoy His grace.

God is affectionate. Your earthly parents may have been cold and distant, but Abba's love toward you is different. He offers affectionate love. When the father reached his son, he "threw his arms around him and kissed him" (Luke 15:20). We also see the affectionate side of God when John lays his head on Jesus' chest during at the Last Supper (see John 13:25).

Rarely do we imagine our heavenly Father as affectionate, particularly if we have grown up with emotionally distant parents. But no matter how emotionally distant your earthly parents were, your heavenly Father is affectionate and longs to express that affection toward you.

God is extravagant. Although your parents may have measured out love to you according to your performance, God's love for you is not like that. He loves you extravagantly, whether you perform well or fail. When the son, who failed miserably, returned home, the father threw an extravagant party in his honor. He spared no expense. Meat was a rare delicacy, but the father ordered the servants to kill a fattened calf for the feast. In other words, he brought out prime rib. He also clothed his son in the most expensive robe he owned.

The apostle John wrote, "How great is the love the Father has lavished on us" (1 John 3:1). When I read this verse, I can't help but think of whipped cream on an ice cream sundae. I love whipped cream and do not use it sparingly—I lavish it on my ice cream sundaes! Our Abba delights to lavish love on us. He spared no expense to demonstrate that love.

Living as a Beloved Daughter

Despite having received Christ's grace for salvation, some of us have never learned to live as though we are His precious and loved daughters. Instead, we wrestle with sinful patterns, trying to muster up enough willpower to change our behavior. We act as if we are servants groping for His approval and trying to earn His favor. We forget that He has given us the Holy Spirit, so we try harder and harder to transform ourselves.

But that is not what God wants; He wants us to sink into His love and live as the beloved daughters we are. When you received God's grace, Jesus gave you His Spirit as a seal of your salvation. You no longer have to try to change yourself. The work of transformation is the Holy Spirit's job. Your job is to simply cooperate with Him. This is why the apostle Paul wrote, "After beginning with the Spirit, are you now trying to attain your goal by human effort?" (Galatians 3:3). When we live our lives by human effort, we live as slaves or servants rather than beloved daughters.

The following lists clarify the differences between living as a daughter and living as a servant. As you read, think about which list best describes how you relate to God.

Characteristics of a Servant

- A servant works to earn approval and therefore is never quite sure she is measuring up.
- A servant views God as distant and addresses Him as "Master."
- A servant defines faith as "trying harder to be better." She relies on willpower for life transformation.
- A servant measures obedience by externals ("Have I read my Bible, given my tithe, and prayed this week?").
- A servant does what's expected but then often struggles with resentment.
- A servant lives in fear of being punished.
- A servant lives with chronic guilt.

Characteristics of a Daughter

- A daughter enjoys full assurance that her Father loves her completely.

- A daughter views God as close and addresses Him with intimate terms such as Abba or Father.
- A daughter defines faith as trusting that she is loved and that God will provide what is best.
- A daughter defines obedience as simply responding to her loving Father.
- A daughter enjoys freedom from fear of her Father's disapproval or wrath.
- A daughter has learned to rely on the Holy Spirit for life transformation. She prays, *Live Your life through me.*
- A daughter lives with steady joy. It's not that she doesn't experience deep sorrow, but she knows she is the sparkle of her Daddy's eye, and that brings a rooted joy that no circumstances can change.

FROM COWERING SERVANT TO BELOVED DAUGHTER

For a long time, I lived as a servant rather than a beloved daughter of Abba. I served God well but had difficulty feeling loved by Him. I couldn't imagine a father like the father in the story—a father I could trust. I wanted to rest in God's love but couldn't imagine God's eyes as loving. The eyes I saw were demanding and harsh. But gradually the Holy Spirit healed old wounds and changed my heart so that now I can honestly say I trust God and feel loved by Him. But in order for that to happen, I had to cooperate with the Holy Spirit and do my part.

First, I reprogrammed my brain by meditating on lots of Scriptures about God's love (see Psalm 130:7; Ephesians 3:16-19). I didn't memorize or meditate on Scripture to please God; I did it so the Holy Spirit could change my thinking and allow me to relax in God's love. I wrote down verses about God's love in my journal and then prayed them back to God, asking Him to open my heart to believing that He loved me that much.

Second, I praised God for His love, even when I didn't feel it. As I was faithful in praising Him, the Holy Spirit increased my faith and trust, and soon I found myself believing that God did love me and that I was indeed precious to Him.

Third, I had to separate my heavenly Father from my earthly father, and I had to change the pictures in my mind. I reminded myself often that my heavenly Father doesn't demand perfection. He doesn't set expectations for me that I can't live up to, and He isn't emotionally distant. He isn't waiting to punish me when I fail. I began to meditate on the father in this story. I spent time imagining what it would be like to come home as that younger son and find a father waiting who wouldn't smack me for coming in late. I imagined what it would be like to come home after failing, only to see compassionate eyes rather than eyes filled with anger. I began to imagine what it would be like to come home to soft, loving, gentle words after I'd messed up rather than to harsh, angry words.

Gradually, the Holy Spirit took the passages I was meditating on, my offering of praise, and the new pictures I was focusing on in my mind and moved the love of God from my head down into my heart.

While those were the primary ways I cooperated with the Holy Spirit as He sought to transform me, I also took some tangible but tiny steps toward trusting God's love.

Baby Steps

I've titled this section "Baby Steps" because just as young children take tiny steps before they become confident in their walking ability, so you will need to take tiny steps toward rebuilding your trust in Abba Father's love. Again, my intent is not to give you more to do; as a performer, your "to-do" list is long enough. My intent is to share with you how God changed me. If He can change me, He can change you, too! Maybe try just one tiny step at a time. As you step forward, the Holy Spirit will enable you to feel the Father's love more. If you stumble and fall, He'll be holding your hand.

Practice coming to God boldly with your hurts. When my daughters or son call me and pour out their hearts, I love it. They share with me the tiniest details of their day and the biggest concerns. Sometimes I hold my breath because I don't want to miss anything. My husband, Steve, is the same. When our kids are hurting, his heart breaks. When they are exuberant, he's thrilled. He loves it when they trust him enough to vent or process with him. He is their father, and he longs to be part of their lives.

Your Abba longs to be part of your life in much the same way. Tell Him everything. Don't hold back, wondering, *Is God really interested in this?* The writer of Hebrews encourages us to "approach the throne of grace with confidence" (4:16) and to "draw near to God with a sincere heart in full assurance of faith" (10:22). Loving parents delight in meeting their children's needs and desires.

Look for characteristics of God in the people you respect. The family of God is one of God's greatest agents of healing grace. He gives us spiritual fathers and mothers who can help heal the wounds from our earthly fathers and mothers.

This has certainly been true for me. I have two older men in my life who I respect deeply. One is my father-in-law, whose godly gentleness affirms me in more ways than I can describe. He reflects the love and affectionate side of Abba. He often hugs me and tells me he loves me. He affirms me for the way God is using the gifts He has given me. My father-in-law might be my biggest fan when it comes to my writing and speaking. He sends me encouraging e-mails and notes and prays for me continually. His faithfulness in my life speaks to me of God's faithfulness.

The other man who has demonstrated characteristics of God to me is Dan Ball. I met Dan during one of the roughest times of my life. He gently came alongside my husband and me, praying for us and encouraging us in our walks with the Lord. I have watched Dan speak gently to his wife, children, and grandchildren. I have heard him speak affirming words to my own kids, encouraging them in their walks with the Lord. His consistency is a picture of God's holiness to me.

Both these men reflect my heavenly Father's love for me. If there are older people in your life who demonstrate godly characteristics, take note of them.

Create visual reminders of God's love. Here are a few ways for how to go about this:

1. Make a scrapbook describing God's love and the characteristics associated with it. Create a page for each attribute: His love, His faithfulness, His gentleness, and so on. Include verses, pictures, poems, and artistic sketches. If you have musical ability, write a song about God as your loving Father and include it in your scrapbook.
2. Put together a Father album of sorts. Many people have baby books that give them a sense of their roots and family. Create your own certificate of adoption. If you remember the date when you accepted Christ as your Savior and became part of God's family, include that. If not, that's okay. Simply confirm that you are God's adopted child. The beauty of an Abba Father scrapbook is that it is something tangible you can return to when you find yourself feeling distant from or fearful of your heavenly Father.

Forgive your earthly parents. Our earthly parents were imperfect and inflicted wounds, some intentionally and some by default. Bitterness and an unforgiving spirit toward them can keep us from experiencing the love and grace of our heavenly Father. When we are harboring bitterness, we often hide from the very One who is able to heal that bitterness. Forgiveness sets us free. As long as you harbor unforgiveness, you are held captive by the people who hurt you.

Forgiveness means you are going to make a conscious decision to let go of the hurts your earthly parents inflicted. Make a list of the ways you were hurt, and then go through that list, telling God that you choose to forgive each offense. After that, burn up or tear up that paper.

God wants you to know Him as a loving Father. He would do anything for you, His precious daughter. Live in the freedom that comes from knowing how deeply you are loved.

Message from the Grace Giver

> My precious child, I love you so much (see 1 John 3:1)! Sink into My love today. I could not love you more than I do at this moment. I love you even when you struggle with sin, even when you are tired or cranky. Listen to the love song I am continually singing over you (see Zephaniah 3:17). You are My beloved child. *Nothing* you do can separate you from My loving presence (see Romans 8:36). I am always available to you and never out of reach. Whenever you feel unloved, come to Me and allow Me to fill your heart with My perfect love.

Praying Scripture to Internalize Grace

Lord God, how I praise You that You have promised to be a loving Father to me! You have called me Your daughter (see 2 Corinthians 6:18). My heart cries with the apostle John, "How great is the love the Father has lavished on us, that we should be called children of God" (1 John 3:1). I have not received a spirit that makes me a slave to fear; I have received the Spirit of "daughtership." It is by Your Spirit that my heart cries, "Abba" (Romans 8:15). Your Spirit now testifies with my spirit that I am God's child (see Romans 8:16). I am no longer to live as a slave to You, but instead I am to live as Your beloved daughter (see Galatians 4:6).

You have loved me with an everlasting love. You pursue and draw me in loving-kindness (see Jeremiah 31:3). How I praise You that nothing, absolutely nothing, can separate me from Your love—not death or life, angels nor demons, the present nor the future, height or depth, or anything else in all creation will be able to separate me from the love of God that is in Christ Jesus my Lord (see Romans 8:38-39). You said, "Greater love has no one than this, that he lay down his life for his friends" (John 15:13). What a friend You are, Lord Jesus! You proved Your love for me by laying down Your life so that I could call You "Abba." Abba, You quiet me, just as a loving father quiets his newborn baby. You sing over me with delight (see Zephaniah 3:17). You call me precious and honored in Your sight because You love me (see Isaiah 43:4).

I praise You that Your love is great. Your faithfulness toward me endures forever (see Psalm 117:2). Your love for me will never change. I never have to feel afraid that I am not good enough for You or that I don't measure up to Your standards. You love me just as I am and sent Your son Jesus to die for my sins so that I never again have to fear not being loved by You. You forgive me and call me worthy because of the death of Your son. How I praise You that You say that I am Your beloved daughter in whom You are well pleased (see Mark 1:11). As Your beloved daughter, I can rest secure (see Deuteronomy 33:12).

A Daily Dose of Grace

Day 1

1. Memorize and meditate on Romans 8:15-16 as written here or in another translation:

   > You did not receive a Spirit of fear that makes you a slave again to fear, but you received the Spirit of sonship. And by him we cry, "*Abba*, Father." The Spirit himself testifies with our spirit that we are God's children.

2. In what ways do you cower in fear before God rather than come to Him confidently as His beloved daughter?

3. How does the Spirit testify with our spirits that we belong to God?

Day 2

1. Read Luke 15:11-32. Make a list of every characteristic of God the Father's heart that is reflected in this story.

2. Read Hebrews 12:2. When the father lifts his robe and runs to greet his younger son (the rebellious one), he humiliates himself in front of the village. How is this a picture of Jesus when He goes to the cross?

3. In the story that Jesus told, the father leaves the banquet and goes to seek reconciliation with the older son, the rule follower. The father goes to "plead with" the older son, not to punish him. What does this reflect about God's heart toward those who are legalistic?

Day 3

This exercise may take some time, so I have given you only one passage and a couple of related questions. I believe that if you take your time and prayerfully complete this exercise, it will be powerful in your life.

1. Read Luke 11:11. In the New King James Version, this verse reads, "If a son asks for bread from any father among you, will he give him a stone? Or if he asks for a fish, will he give him a serpent instead of a fish?" If a "stone" represents emotional coldness, and a "serpent" represents abuse, either verbal or physical, how could these "gifts" from your earthly parents confuse your thinking about your heavenly Father?

2. Compare your earthly parents with your heavenly Father. Look up Scriptures that describe your heavenly Father and meditate on those. For example:

Earthly Parents	*Heavenly Father*
cold / distant	compassionate / loving (Psalm 103:8)

Day 4

1. Read Psalm 13:5-6. What do these verses teach you about God's love?

2. Read Psalm 17:6-8. How does listening to our prayers demonstrate God's love toward us?

3. Read Psalm 48:9. When we meditate on something, it simply means we fix our minds on that thing. We rehearse that truth over and over again in our minds. How can meditating on God's love help move the truth of His love from your head down to your heart?

Day 5

1. Read Galatians 4:6-7. Rewrite these verses substituting the word *daughter* for *son*. How is living as a daughter different from living as a slave?

2. Take an honest look at your life. Do you live more as a servant or as a daughter of God? What would it take for you to live with more of an awareness that God is your loving Father?

3. Read Isaiah 52:2. If you really believed that God was your loving Father, how would that free you from the chains that hold you captive?

Day 6

1. Review Romans 8:15-16.

2. What baby steps (see page 155) do you need to take to rebuild your trust in God's love for you?

3. On the next page, write a prayer of praise to your heavenly Father for the qualities He has that your earthly parents did not have. Address your prayer to Abba as a reminder that He is your Daddy.

Dear Abba,

CHAPTER 9

WALK AWAY FROM THE BAIT

It is inevitable that, in a world of increasing harshness and cruelty, you will at some point be hurt. But if you fail to react with love and forgiveness, if you retain in your spirit the debt the offender owes you, that offense will rob your heart of its capacity to love.

FRANCIS FRANGIPANE

I felt so offended. The fellow staff member's words stung: "Becky, women's ministries doesn't need a paid staff position. At its peak, the program was run by a volunteer!" I replayed the words in my mind and then built my defense. I thought about all the good things I had brought to our women's ministries program: leadership, training, a women's morning Bible study, a heart for the hurting, creative outreach. The program was growing and lives were being changed. Had this man not noticed? How could he say that women's ministries had gone better under a volunteer's leadership? My performer's heart was crushed! I vacillated between hurt, anger, self-doubt, and the desire to prove him wrong.

The more I obsessed, the worse I felt. Later that morning, I read these words written by the psalmist David: "Free me from the trap that is set for me" (Psalm 31:4). That's when it hit me: I had taken the bait. Ugh! And Satan had me exactly where he wanted me: trapped!

As part of my research for this book, I asked women why it is so easy for performers to become offended. I received some great answers. Here are just a few:

- "We do so poorly with criticism because it pokes a hole in our false self (perfection). When someone criticizes us, we panic. We become swallowed in fear because we think they have seen us for what we truly are. We are panicked that they have discovered that we are imperfect and that we will no longer be loved, accepted, valued, and praised because we aren't perfect. In one fell swoop, they have stripped from us our only hope of achieving love, and we will fight with everything in us to fix that hole they poked into our mask. We'll show them. And so we dance better, strive harder, and keep up the show even though we are exhausted and just long for someone to love us, faults and all."
- "When I am criticized, I get offended because it's a knee-jerk reaction that is really covering up how exposed and vulnerable I feel in that moment. There is definitely a sense of anxiety and panic, and my thoughts obsess on how I can fix this and maintain the facade I've been living under."
- "I'm a people pleaser. To be criticized means I failed or let someone down in some way. I also think many performers take offense where perhaps none was intended, as we're looking for approval. If our efforts are overlooked and we don't receive the positive feedback we need and crave, we feel offended."

It seems that we performers are easily offended for one of two reasons: We have been criticized or our efforts have been ignored.

Satan knows exactly how to trap us. He too longed for stardom, and he knows just how to bait us. He dangles before us hurt feelings from being criticized, ignored, or slighted. Once we take offense, snap! The trap closes and we're caught. Satan sits back and laughs because he knows that once we're offended, it's harder to win us over than conquering a strong city (see Proverbs 18:9).

Jesus told a story for every performer who is easily offended. Peter had asked Jesus, "Lord, how many times shall I forgive my brother when he sins against me? Up to seven times?" In response, Jesus replied, "I tell you, not seven times, but seventy-seven times" (Matthew 18:21-22), and then He told the following story to underscore the importance of extending grace to others even when they offend us (see verses 23-35).

The Parable of the Unmerciful Servant

One day a king decided to settle his accounts and balance his books. In order to do this, he called in a servant who owed him ten thousand talents, which was the equivalent to twenty million dollars in today's money.[1] However, the servant was not able to pay back the amount he owed. (No surprise there! Who could pay back such a debt?) So the king ordered the servant, his wife, and his children to sell all their possessions in order to repay the debt. Now, that may seem harsh to us, but this directive was in accordance to the custom of the day.

When the servant heard this, he fell to his knees and begged for more time to pay off his debt. Note that he did not ask that the debt be forgiven, just for more time. The master knew it was humanly impossible for the servant to pay back such a huge amount, so he took pity on the servant and cancelled the entire debt.

After receiving such a generous gift, what the servant did next was unimaginable. He went to a fellow servant (a man of the same social standing as himself) who owed him one hundred denarii, which in today's dollars would have been about twenty dollars. He choked his fellow servant and demanded that he pay his debt. The fellow servant begged for more time, but the forgiven servant refused and had his fellow servant thrown into prison. Some other servants were watching the whole scenario and reported the ungrateful servant to the master.

When the master summoned the servant, he called him wicked and rebuked him for not extending the same forgiveness to his fellow servant. The master then had the unmerciful servant thrown into prison to be tortured. At this point, Jesus threw in the punch line: "This is how my heavenly Father will treat each of you unless you forgive your brother from your heart" (Matthew 18:35).

Now you might be wondering, *Torture? What's up with that? That doesn't seem to fit with God's offer of grace!* Does this parable teach that if we don't forgive, God is going to torture us? Because of what the rest of Scripture teaches, we know God's acceptance is based on receiving His grace.[2]

What Jesus Meant

As I have studied and asked God for wisdom as to how to interpret this part of the parable, I have come to believe that if we have truly experienced God's forgiveness, we will choose to offer forgiveness to others. If we don't offer forgiveness to others, God often allows us to experience harsh discipline in order that we might comply with His will. In addition, I believe that we experience emotional torture when we take Satan's bait. No one else has to torture us; when we take offense, we become bitter and are tormented by their own thoughts. We rehearse over and over in our minds the wrong done to us. Our torture might include obsessing about getting revenge or proving the other person wrong. Before we know it, we are trapped in bitterness.

This is what has happened with Evelyn. She sits in her apartment day after day, living the life of a recluse. Years ago, her children offended her by making accusations about abuse in the family. Evelyn will never forgive her children for their accusations. Instead, she has chosen bitterness. She considers herself a victim and obsesses about ways to prove that her kids are wrong. She sits at home and stews over how unfair life has treated her. She fills her hours watching meaningless TV shows and escaping into shallow novels. The sad thing is that Evelyn has so much to offer the world, but by reassuring herself that she is "right," she is wasting her later years with a bitter heart.

In *Rewriting Your Emotional Script*, I defined *bitterness* as "the monument we build to our pain."[3] We might not become a recluse as Evelyn did, but bitterness can be expressed in other ways:

- We might rehearse the criticism over and over and sink into a pit of despair.
- We might work hard to prove that we are worthwhile.
- We might lose the joy of God's grace by fixating on how to get revenge.
- We might try to overcompensate in order to prove that our offender's opinions toward us are not valid. As a result, we begin living out of the false self.
- We feel hurt and that we deserve better.
- Our thoughts become self-focused, and we feel as though our situation is just too hard for others to understand.
- We become judgmental and critical of the other person.

Ultimately, when we take Satan's bait, we feel we are owed a debt, just like the servant in Jesus' story. Dear offended one, there is another way.

GRACE GLIMPSE

Grace offers me the option to not take Satan's bait.

The Greek word for offense is *skandalon*, from which we get the word *scandal*. "It was originally the name of the part of a trap to which the bait is attached, hence, the trap or snare itself."[4] Satan uses the offense as bait, tempting us toward bitterness because he knows if he can get us to embrace bitterness, we will not experience God's grace to the fullest extent.

As long as we live in a fallen world, he will continue to dangle the bait of offense. But the exciting truth is that we don't have to take the bait!

Don't Take the Bait

Before I take offense at something, I have found it helpful to step back and ask some simple questions. These questions slow down my reaction time and enable me with the help of the Holy Spirit to examine my heart so that I don't become bitter and miss enjoying God's grace. The writer of Hebrews penned, "See to it that no one misses the grace of God and that no bitter root grows up to cause trouble and defile many" (12:15). I don't want to miss the grace of God, nor do I want to be defiled by bitterness. So when I'm tempted to take offense, I ask the Holy Spirit to help me answer these five questions:

1. What is the truth in this situation? Jesus promised that the Holy Spirit would guide us to truth. When I am in performer mode, it is easy to exaggerate the hurt and lose perspective. While I don't always trust myself, I can always trust the Holy Spirit because He never loses perspective. When I ask for His help to see the truth, He may show me that:

- This person's opinion of me does not change God's opinion of me.
- This person most likely had no intention of hurting me. He or she might just be having a bad day or might not have communicated well. For example, in the opening story of this

chapter, my fellow staff member did not intend to hurt me; he was just concerned with the church budget.

- If I am being criticized, I might need to improve in some area. It's not that I want to get back into performance mode, but the Holy Spirit might lead me to correct or improve my skills in some area of my life. For example, once during a radio interview, I said something that so upset a listener that he wrote to the station. I was able to ask the Holy Spirit what the truth was, and He helped me see that I could have communicated what I was trying to say more effectively. The Holy Spirit showed me not to get uptight but to communicate my point differently next time.
- This person's opinion of me does not determine the validity of God's calling on my life. Only God has that right.

2. Is there a trigger involved? A trigger is something that reminds us of a past hurt. For example, it's possible that in your childhood, you were ridiculed for your lack of ability in some area. The hurt may have gone so deep that you don't even remember what happened. When someone criticizes your performance in that area, it might trigger the same response you had in childhood. Perhaps you either withdraw or recoil and get ready to strike back.

Jesus called the Holy Spirit the counselor (see John 16:7), so I ask Him as my counselor to show me triggers I might not see myself. If He shows me one, I ask Him to heal that wounded place of my heart. The Holy Spirit delights to answer this prayer.

3. Why is this so important to me? Sometimes when I am tempted to take offense, I need to ask myself, *What's going on inside of me? Why is this so important to me?* We may lack self-awareness because our self-protective instincts are so strong. This is why the psalmist David wrote, "Search me, O God, and know my heart; test me and know my anxious thoughts. See if there is any offensive way in me"

(Psalm 139:23-24). Sometimes our "offensive way" is when we feel offended by someone else. When I ask the Holy Spirit to search my heart and show me the motivation behind my hurt feelings, He might show me that I want to feel more valued or significant. Or He might show me that my motivation is to be the center of attention. Once I see my motivation, I ask the Holy Spirit to heal my heart and reassure me of His love and approval.

4. Is God trying to teach me something? In the journey to find freedom from performance, God may gently remind me that my pride needs to be uprooted. One way to do this is through criticism from a friend, coworker, or spouse. The Holy Spirit's main concern is my soul transformation (see Ephesians 4:23-24; Romans 8:10-11). When a person criticizes my performance, it provides a wonderful opportunity for God to re-teach me the lesson that my identity cannot rest in my accomplishments but in His grace alone. Whether there is truth to the person's words is irrelevant. God wants me to find my identity solely in His grace and not in how well I perform.

5. Do I need to lay down my expectations? Oh, this is essential! As performers, we generally have expectations of others that are too high or unrealistic. Part of maturing in Christ and letting go of the need to perform is realizing that the world does not revolve around us. We don't need to be the center of attention in order to feel valuable; instead, we are to have the same attitude as Christ, who had the attitude of a servant and was completely humble (see Philippians 2:5-7). At times, our friends and family are going to ignore us or forget our needs. Our relationships are going to change, and we might have to lay down our expectations in that process.

This is often the case with moms and daughters. For instance, when a daughter gets married, her relationship with her mother changes. This is healthy, right, and good. However, it can be an adjustment for you as a mom when the daughter you felt so close to forgets your birthday or doesn't call as much. She might be so wrapped up in her children's activities that she forgets to send a thank-you note. I have talked with countless mothers who are having difficulty adjusting to changing seasons. Before you take Satan's bait and try to guilt your daughter, ask the Holy Spirit to show you how to lay down your expectations.

Typically, if I step back and ask myself those five questions, with the Holy Spirit's help, I can walk away from the bait. But what if you've already taken the bait and realize you are trapped? How do you escape?

An Escape Plan

I love a good plan, don't you? Most performers do. I'll keep it simple: Cancel the debt and pray that your offender will be blessed.

Cancel the debt. Jesus taught His disciples to pray, "Forgive us our debts, as we also have forgiven our debtors" (Matthew 6:12). When you extend grace by canceling another person's debt, you are the beneficiary of that grace because the Holy Spirit pushes the truth of God's grace down deeper into your heart.

To cancel the debt, first write out how you have been offended. Then write down why you took offense. Tell the Lord that you forgive your offender and that you want to cancel the debt. Then with a red marker write, "Cancelled!" over both. Immediately, without hesitating, move to the next step, whether you feel like it or not.

Pray that the one who offended you is blessed. The more quickly I begin this practice, the less likely I am to walk back to the bait. Any time the offense comes back to mind, I release it to the Lord again and immediately begin praying that my offender will be blessed. After Job's friends offended him, God invited him to pray that his friends would be blessed (see Job 42:8-10). When he did, God actually blessed Job!

When I have prayed Scripture on behalf of the person who offended me, I have found that I am far less likely to hold on to the offense. Let me give you a few examples of verses I have prayed (put the person's name in the blanks):

- *Lord, I pray that ______________ would be filled with the spirit of wisdom and revelation so that ________________ might know You more fully and rest more in the hope to which he/she has been called.* (see Ephesians 1:7-8)
- *Lord Jesus, I pray that ________________ would be strengthened through the Holy Spirit to know how wide and long and high and deep Your love is for him/her.* (see Ephesians 3:16-18)
- *Father, I pray that You would do more than what ____________________ is able to ask or imagine. I pray that Your power would be alive in his/her life.* (see Ephesians 3:20)

All of these Scriptures are from the book of Ephesians, but you can use any Scripture to pray that the person who hurt you will be blessed. As you pray that the person is blessed, *you* will be blessed in return. It's so worth it!

Live Debt-Free

As we bring this chapter to a close, I want you to know that I've been praying for you. This offense stuff is tough! Your freedom depends to a large degree on whether you take Satan's bait. Choose wisely. Commit to God that from now on, with the help of the Holy Spirit, you are going to ask yourself the five questions before you take Satan's bait. It can be helpful to write your commitment in a journal and sign and date that commitment.

Then ask the Lord to show you relationships that are strained because you've taken the bait. Resolve through the power of the Holy Spirit to let that offense go and cancel the debt. When you refuse to cancel the debt, you end up living in bondage to your anger and hurt.

Ultimately, it creates a debt for you. So the time is now to cancel those debts. Write down your resolution and date it. Then immediately, without hesitation, begin praying that the person who offended you will be blessed. God will bless you beyond what you can imagine as you choose to live a debt-free life.

Message from the Grace Giver

> My child, I came to set you free (see Galatians 5:1). When you are tempted to take offense, stand firm in your freedom. Don't let Satan trap you! I will always provide a way out (see 1 Corinthians 10:13). I live within you and am present with you continually. When you feel tempted to take the bait, stop and ask Me to strengthen you. I will show you the way out. The surest way to avoid Satan's bait is to sink deeply into My love. If you grow in your understanding of how high and deep and wide My love is for you, it will become easier to not take offense because you will know that at the deepest level, you do not have to prove yourself to Me. If I correct you, it will always be because I love you and want what's best for you (see Hebrews 12:5-6).

Praying Scripture to Internalize Grace

I give You thanks, Father God, because You give me victory through Your Son, Jesus Christ (see 1 Corinthians 15:57). I don't need to fear Satan's schemes because greater is the One in me than the one who is in the world (see 1 John 4:4). I praise You because through Your death and resurrection, You triumphed over the evil one and all his schemes.

Lord Jesus, You said, "Away from me, Satan!" (Matthew 4:10). Teach me to follow Your example. You promise that if I faithfully resist the Devil, he will flee from me (see James 4:7). When I am tempted by Satan's bait, help me to step back and lean into the wisdom that the

Holy Spirit provides so that I can think clearly and not react.

Your Word tells me to prepare my mind for action, be self-controlled, and set my hope fully on the grace given to me by Jesus Christ (see 1 Peter 1:13). It teaches that if I forgive an offense, I will promote love in my relationships, but if I take offense, I will separate even my close friends (see Proverbs 17:9). Help me to treasure my relationships and to offer others the grace You have offered me. Teach me to live harmoniously with others, being sympathetic, loving, compassionate, and humble. Help me not to repay evil with evil or insult with insult, but show me how to pray blessing even over those who sometimes offend me (see 1 Peter 3:8-9).

So, Lord Jesus, I commit my sensitive spirit to You. When Satan baits me, I will choose to walk away so that he will not outwit me (see 2 Corinthians 2:11). I praise You that You always lead me in triumphal procession in Christ, and through me You spread the fragrance of the knowledge of Jesus (see 2 Corinthians 2:14).

A Daily Dose of Grace

Day 1

1. Memorize and meditate on Proverbs 19:11 as written here or in another translation:

   > A [woman's] wisdom gives [her] patience; it is to [her] glory to overlook an offense.

2. Think about the words written in Proverbs 19:11. If you lack wisdom, how can you get some (see James 1:5)?

3. How is God's grace glorified (made to look bigger) in our lives if we overlook offenses?

Day 2

1. Read the parable of the unmerciful servant in Matthew 18:23-35. Why do you think Jesus placed such a priority on not taking offense?

2. Do you think offering others grace impacts your ability to experience God's grace? Why, or why not?

Day 3

1. Read Proverbs 17:9 and 18:19. According to these two verses, what are the benefits of not taking offense?

2. Luke 17:1 says, "It is impossible that no offenses should come" (NKJV). How does Satan use an offense to trap us?

3. Read 2 Corinthians 2:11. If we take offense, how does Satan outwit us?

Day 4

1. Read Hebrews 12:14-15. What do these verses teach about the correlation between bitterness and missing out on the significance that is ours in God's grace?

2. How do you think bitterness prevents us from internalizing God's grace?

3. Do you find yourself becoming offended easily? If you realized God's grace, do you think it would help you not take offense so easily?

Day 5

1. Think back on the last time someone offended you. Write about that situation in the space provided.

2. Read 1 Peter 3:8-9. What does it look like for you to offer grace? What tangible step can you take to offer grace to the person who offended you? Write a prayer, expressing your desire to forgive.

3. Write a prayer of blessing for the offending individual. Use the Scriptures listed on page 174 or some Scriptures of your own choosing.

Day 6

1. Review Proverbs 19:11. Why do you think letting go of offenses is such an important step in your freedom?

2. Go for a walk and spend some time praising God for the freedom He offers through His grace. If worship music helps you focus your thoughts, take your worship music along and celebrate the freedom that Christ offers you. You don't have to live your life trapped by Satan!

CHAPTER 10

SURRENDER IN THE HIDDEN PLACE

God's servants must be taught the value of the hidden life.

F. B. MEYER

"The earth was formless and empty, and darkness was over the surface of the deep, and the Spirit of God was hovering over the waters" (Genesis 1:2). *Formless and empty.* Steve played the words over in his mind, and they seemed to echo through his soul. Just a few weeks before, my husband had resigned, under pressure, from a prominent pastoral position. Overnight he'd gone from a place of influence to a place of obscurity. His life came to a screeching halt.

Steve's hopes and dreams had crashed, leaving a wake of depression and uncertainty. Would God ever use him again? Would He ever restore him to the type of leadership position he had enjoyed in the past? Like many others who unexpectedly enter the hidden place, he felt empty and afraid.

In the days following Steve's resignation, the Holy Spirit led him to read the book of Genesis. He had read Genesis 1 hundreds of times before, but this time the phrase *formless and empty* struck a chord in his heart. That morning, he wrote in his journal,

> The earth was empty, a formless mass, cloaked in darkness. And the Spirit of God was hovering over its waters.
>
> Father, I feel like my vocational life is empty—a formless mass, cloaked in darkness. I confess that I just can't see the future of my ministry with any kind of clarity whatsoever. It's formless and void. I rejoice that Your Spirit is hovering over the waters. . . . Give me a renewed sense of anticipation, O Lord! Give me a feeling of expectation. Reassure me that the best is yet to come. You are hovering over me right now.[1]

The months that followed were the hardest of our lives, but they were also transformative, especially for Steve. During that time, he spent hours alone with God. God reassured him that He loved him and that His love for him wasn't based on his performance. Though our circumstances did not change, Steve did.

He no longer finds his identity in being a megachurch pastor but in being a beloved child of God. He no longer measures success in churches by programs, plates, and pews. He would now tell you that a "win" is a life transformed. He's far more compassionate and a better listener. He's more of a servant and less concerned with image. He's more leisurely in his time with the Lord and less driven.

We are now back serving a church, and Steve's ministry is more fruitful. His sphere of influence has grown. He is consulted often for advice. He's back to speaking at conferences both nationally and internationally. The time spent in the hidden place transformed both his life and his ministry because there, in what felt like a tomb, Steve learned two life-changing lessons: When God strips it all away, He gives Himself. And when one's dreams die, it's time for God's resurrecting power!

This is the message of the parable of the grain of wheat. Let's take a look.

THE PARABLE OF A GRAIN OF WHEAT

Jesus said, "I tell you the truth, unless a kernel of wheat falls to the ground and dies, it remains only a single seed. But if it dies, it produces many seeds. The man who loves his life will lose it, while the man who hates his life in this world will keep it for eternal life" (John 12:24-25). Jesus spoke these words when His public ministry was winding down. He knew that His disciples would have difficulty understanding what was about to happen, so in this tiny parable, He spoke prophetically about His death and resurrection. From a human perspective, after Christ's death, His ministry would look like one big fizzle—as though He were a failure. Wasn't He supposed to usher in the kingdom? Dying and being buried hardly fit the disciple's definition of success. But through His death, burial, and resurrection, Jesus would make it possible for the redemption of humankind.

Jesus went on to say that only those willing to lose their lives will be redeemed. There is an important and yet hard principle here for the performer.

GRACE GLIMPSE

In the hidden place, the place of obscurity, grace calls me to bury my dreams. Only then am I able to embrace God's resurrecting power.

Unless a grain of wheat dies and is buried in the ground, it cannot become a blade of wheat that produces many more grains. Similarly, Christ invites us to die to ourselves and embrace the life He offers. Just as buried grain brings forth much fruit, so our lives bring forth an abundance of fruit as we surrender them in exchange for Christ's life.

This is hard, especially for performers! It is so difficult to let go of our dreams, and it can feel excruciating to watch them die. But when our dreams die, it's time for a resurrection! When we are willing to lose our life for Christ's, the fruitfulness He brings is more than we could ever imagine. It might be different than we thought, but the lasting effect will be beyond what we could have hoped. The apostle Paul echoed this principle, having written, "What you sow does not come to life unless it dies" (1 Corinthians 15:36).

Most of us would rather be seen and acknowledged. Let's face it: Performers love to be the center of attention. We would rather feel successful and influential. Suffering and sorrow often require us to pull away from everything and sink into the Almighty. This is why the hidden place is so important in our transformation. There, in our aloneness, we begin to understand that we must allow Christ to be all; He will not share the stage.

We may feel forgotten in this place, but nothing could be further from the truth. We are not forgotten; we have simply entered the hidden place. The hidden place feels like a tomb. It is a place where activity, applause, accomplishment, and affirmation are all absent. There, hidden away from the applause of the world, God performs deep soul surgery and we are transformed and become more like Christ.

Jesus Himself spent time in the hidden place. We see this reflected in John 13–21. His public ministry over, Jesus moved into a time of obscurity: little or no activity, no applause, no affirmation, and seemingly no accomplishment. He experienced loneliness (see 16:32), betrayal (see 18:2-3), rejection (see 18:17,25-26), suffering (see 19:1-4,17-18), and ultimately death (see 18:30). Like the grain of wheat, He was buried in the ground. But that's not the end of the story.

Here is our hope: Out of that hidden place, He arose victorious over sin and death and hell. The most fruitful part of Jesus' ministry came out of the hidden place. His death and resurrection set Him apart and compel us to bow because

> God exalted him to the highest place
> and gave him the name that is above every name,

> that at the name of Jesus every knee should bow,
> in heaven and on earth and under the earth,
> and every tongue confess that Jesus Christ is Lord.
> (Philippians 2:9-11)

If you want freedom from performance, you must consider Christ's call to die. You will most likely spend time in the hidden place, where He will use sorrow and suffering to transform you and make you more like Jesus. I'm not saying run after sorrow or suffering. That would be crazy! I'm simply saying that when those times come, recognize that God can use them to transform you and free you from your need for applause.

TRANSFORMED IN THE HIDDEN PLACE

The hidden place is crucial to our transformation for several reasons:

In the hidden place, our focus changes. "Set your hearts on things above" (Colossians 3:1). As performers, we are tempted to try to fix ourselves. In the hidden place, where success, influence, and affirmation are absent, our focus changes. We stop trying so hard to fix ourselves and instead lift our thoughts to Jesus and ask Him to fix us. We stop clamoring after approval, success, and influence and instead put our trust in God's grace alone, recognizing that we can do nothing to earn His favor. His grace is a gift, pure and simple (see Romans 6:23).

Trusting God is hard, particularly in the hidden place, where we are tempted to doubt His goodness and the consistency of His love. Henri Nouwen believed that this is part of why the hidden place is so important. At the pinnacle of his teaching career at one of the most influential universities in the country, Nouwen accepted a call to work with the intellectually challenged of our society: those who were marginalized because they were mentally handicapped. Quicker than most could imagine, he moved from the place of influence to obscurity.

He wrote,

> One of the reasons that hiddenness is such an important aspect of the spiritual life is that it keeps us focused on God. In hiddenness we do not receive human acclamation, admiration, support, or encouragement. In hiddenness we have to go to God with our sorrows . . . and trust that God will give us what we most need.[2]

In the hidden place, egoism dies. “You died, and your life is now hidden with Christ in God” (Colossians 3:3). When you come to Christ to receive His grace, there is an element of dying (not physical but spiritual) because in that moment, you are identifying yourself with Christ’s death on the cross. This is why Paul wrote, “I have been crucified with Christ and I no longer live, but Christ lives in me” (Galatians 2:20). Even though we were crucified with Christ, we still need to die to self every day. Dying to self can feel confusing. We don’t die to our personality or to the gifts God has given us. In the words of Dr. Catherine Hart Weber, “What we die to is our selfish, unredeemed, lower sinful nature. We instead nurture and cultivate the positive goodness and higher nature of the Holy Spirit in us. We put to death our ‘earthy nature’—by not feeding it.”[3] In order for the life of Christ to be formed in us, we must continually choose to let go of the old and embrace the new life we have in Christ.

This dying to self happens best away from accomplishment and applause because affirmation from others feeds our false self. The more our false self is fed, the more we can build our self-worth on the wrong things. Our egos have a ravenous appetite to be fed. God will often draw us into the hidden place so that our ego becomes starved. In its anorexic state, it begins to feed slowly and solely on God’s grace. Those who die to self are those who “urgently need the Lord. They come to Him daily in empty-handed spiritual need, feeding on His grace in their hearts."[4] When we are hidden away, rather than feeding our identity with the applause and affirmation of others, we are humbled and forced to feed on God's grace alone.

Does dying to self mean that we don't practice self-care? No. Dying to self is surrendering to God's plans for your life. Henri Nouwen wrote, "To die to self requires the death of what has become so precious to you: influence, success and yes, often affection and praise."[5] It means dying to your false self—the self that is built on accomplishments, activities, and the applause of others. It involves daily turning away from the temptation to find your worth and value in anything other than Jesus Christ and His grace in your life.

As we talked about in chapter 4, godly self-care involves nurturing and cultivating your soul so that you are more able to grow and cultivate your life in the Spirit. This includes taking care of your body (which is the sanctuary of the Spirit), taking care of your emotions (which are to reflect the Lord Jesus Christ), and taking care of your soul (the part of you that craves relationship with God).

In the hidden place, we are purified. "Put to death, therefore, whatever belongs to your earthly nature" (Colossians 3:5). How do we put to death what belongs to our earthly nature? We continually surrender ourselves to God and His plans for our lives. The hidden place provides the perfect setting. Trials often force us to surrender, and the end result is refinement (see Isaiah 48:10). When unexpected trials enter our lives, they generally reveal the condition of our souls. If our egos have been fed with applause and affirmation, pride is inevitable. God knows that pride will prevent us from the full experience of His grace. He uses the hidden place to purify our hearts from pride and from envy, greed, idolatry, and a host of other sins (see Colossians 3:3-5). Ruth Myers wrote, "As fire melts unrefined silver, bringing the impurities to the surface, so trials bring the 'scum' to the top in your life."[6] The hidden place becomes a crucible of transformation, and a natural purifying takes place.

Melissa found this to be true in her hidden place. When she was unexpectedly diagnosed with a brain tumor the size of a tangerine, her thriving, productive life came to a screeching halt. Months after brain surgery, she still couldn't drive. She had to let go of her business and much of her independence. After so many losses, Melissa gave in to depression. Daily, she cried out to God, at times sobbing for His grace. I recently talked with Melissa and asked her how it was going. She says that though it's been incredibly difficult, she doesn't tend to measure her worth in terms of productivity anymore. She's become more patient with the suffering of others and less quick to form judgments. Her faith in God has also been purified because it has stood the test of suffering.

The apostle Peter understood how God uses suffering and sorrow to purify our faith. When speaking of trials, he wrote, "These have come so that your faith—of greater worth than gold, which perishes even though refined by fire—may be proved genuine" (1 Peter 1:7). Our faith is proved genuine and of great value when it survives the test of suffering and sorrow.

In the hidden place, we rediscover the all-sufficiency of Jesus Christ. "Christ is all" (Colossians 3:11). In our great weakness, His grace is strong, and we discover He really is enough. We may find ourselves crying, *I don't have the strength to endure this trial. May I borrow Your strength, dear Jesus?* This is a prayer that God loves to answer. I know because I've prayed it many times.

The apostle Paul wrote, "God is able to make all grace abound to you" (2 Corinthians 9:8). Paul pleaded with the Lord many times to take away what he called his "thorn in the flesh." We don't know what that thorn was, but we do know it was a source of sorrow to Paul. Thorns hurt! Though he begged to be released from his thorn, God answered, "My grace is sufficient for you, for my power is made perfect in weakness" (12:9).

I have found this to be true in my life as well. In the months after

Steve resigned, doctors found a tumor on one of my ovaries. Not only was I worried about fighting cancer again, I was also worried about my husband and our lack of income, dealing with memories about my sexual abuse, and walking through some depression. I was going to many doctor's appointments as well as counseling appointments. I found myself missing my public life, because that's where the applause came. The pressure of the trials I was experiencing felt so intense, there were days I did not know if I would survive, nor if I wanted to survive! I had to withdraw—just me and the Lord—to process all that was going on. I crawled away with Him and hid for a while. Some days I lay on the floor reading my Bible and listening to praise music; other days I went for long walks and asked God to reveal more of Himself to me through nature. In the hidden place, I discovered a rare treasure: the beauty of His precious presence. I can now say that Jesus is all-sufficient. He is enough. I'm not sure I could have said that before. When life is going well, it's so easy to say that Jesus is enough, but hidden away in His presence, I was transformed.

WHAT TRANSFORMATION LOOKS LIKE

When we are transformed, we are changed—changed so that we look more like Jesus.

We reflect His heart (see Colossians 3:12-14). Though we don't transform ourselves, we can choose to cooperate with the Holy Spirit in our transformational process by receiving and putting on compassion, kindness, humility, gentleness, and patience. God not only offers us these new attributes, He promises to empower us to live them out.

Let's take a closer look at each of these, along with an example of a simple prayer you can pray to underscore the idea of Christ living out these qualities through you.

- *Compassion.* Compassion speaks of sensitivity to the needs and feelings of others. It is the ability to enter someone else's pain. This is, after all, what Christ did for us. Those who have suffered and spent some time in the hidden place tend to reenter the world with a more compassionate heart. As they have experienced the comfort of Christ, they are able to offer that to others. *Lord, pour Your compassion through me.*

- *Kindness.* When we respond with generosity toward others, we express the kindness of God toward them. After being tucked away, we become so grateful for the grace God has showered on us that we discover the sheer joy of being kind to others (see Galatians 5:22). *Lord, show Your kindness through me. Help my family, coworkers, and neighbors see Your kindness in me.*
- *Humility.* Andrew Murray says it this way: In "humility we have the mystery of grace, which teaches us that as we lose ourselves in the overwhelming greatness of redeeming love, humility becomes to us the consummation of everlasting blessedness and adoration."[7] The more we lose ourselves in Christ, the more He lives His life out through us. *Lord, live Your humility through me. Help me not to try to prove my significance today but instead rest in You and live humbly, as You did.*
- *Gentleness.* I can always tell when a person has spent much time in the hidden place, alone with God, because he or she reflects a gentleness that can be developed only in the presence of Christ. It is as if the suffering and sorrow chisel away any hard edges that might have been there. What remains is a soft gentleness. "I will give you a new heart and put a new spirit in you; I will remove from you your heart of stone and give you a heart of flesh" (Ezekiel 36:26). *Lord, let others experience Your gentleness through me.*
- *Patience.* In the hidden place, life feels slow. At first this may feel exasperating, but the weaning off of activity produces patience. The Greek word that Paul uses here could be translated "longsuffering." It carries the idea of demonstrating patience or putting up with people who irritate.[8] Again, the woman who

has spent considerable time in the hidden place has allowed the grace of God to cover over the unexpected irritants in her life, and thus the beauty of patience has developed. *Lord, demonstrate Your patience through me.*

- *Love.* As we spend time hidden away in Christ, a holy union develops. We become one with Christ (see 1 Corinthians 6:17). We become one with the One who is love (see 1 John 4:7). As a result, we become more loving. *Lord, love others through me.*

We express His peace (see Colossians 3:15). Those who have been transformed by the hidden place have made peace with the sorrow and suffering that God has allowed in their lives. They are no longer fighting to have a "perfect life." They have come to realize that God can bring good out of any evil (see Romans 8:28).

I have noticed that peaceful look in others. It's the peace that comes after struggling, wrestling, and weeping alone with God. It's the deep, settled awareness that He has allowed suffering and sorrow. We may not understand, but we can rest because His grace is more than sufficient.

My friend Karen has this peace. She has endured radiation and chemo for cancer, the loss of her hair, and feeling sicker than a dog. Yet, in spite of how hard it's been, she has allowed the peace of Christ to rule in her heart. She wrote me and told me that God has been faithful through every past trial and that she felt a peace that was beyond understanding because she knew she could trust God's grace to be sufficient in her life this time as well. Where did that peace come from? I believe that it came from extended time in the hidden place, tucked away in the presence of the Lord.

We crave His Word (see Colossians 3:16). Both Steve and I discovered in the hidden place that we no longer felt *obligated* to spend time in God's Word—we became *desperate* to do so. We came to His Word hungry every morning, longing for Him to speak to us, to sustain us.

We meditated and memorized, not because someone told us we should but because His Word was life. When we felt we could not go on, we turned to His Word. When we felt there was no hope, we opened our Bibles. When we felt God had forgotten us, we rehearsed His promises. The more we craved Him, the more He satisfied.

If you are presently in the hidden place, dive into the Bible. I promise you, you will emerge from the hidden place transformed, with a hunger for His Word that you can't explain to others.

Sovereign Grace

Ultimately, the path to freedom leads us to die to whatever we have previously clung to as our source of significance. There in the tomb of the hidden place we bury our hopes and dreams and we surrender. Only then are we able to experience the power of the Resurrection!

Shortly after Steve resigned, we had lunch with a friend and fellow pastor. I will never forget what he told Steve: "Until you admit that God orchestrated your crucifixion, you will not be able to heal. Just as He orchestrated the crucifixion of His own Son, so His sovereign grace arranged yours." Those were tough words to hear at the time, but they are true words. You see, it's almost as if Christ beckons us from the cross, inviting us to come and join Him. He knows that when we have been crucified with Him, we exchange what we formerly clung to as "our life" for Christ's life (see Galatians 2:20). He becomes our "hope of glory" (Colossians 1:27). In the end, as author Brennan Manning describes it, "the Christ within who is our hope of glory is not a matter of theological debate or philosophical speculation. He is not a hobby, a part-time project, a good theme for a book or a last resort when all human effort fails. He is our life, the most real fact about us. He is the power and wisdom of God dwelling within us."[9]

If you are in the tomb of the hidden place, get down on your knees and bow before His sovereign grace. God has allowed you to be crucified with His beloved Son so that He might resurrect new life in you and set you free from the driving desire to find your life in anything other than Him.

Message from the Grace Giver

> My precious one, don't despise the place of obscurity. Watching your dreams die is hard. I know that you crave attention and applause, but as you learn to surrender in the hidden place, I will transform and resurrect you. Don't fight what I am trying to accomplish in your life. Stop trying to arrange your own escape from the hidden place. Instead, surrender and exchange your life for Mine. There in the tomb My grace will transform you into the image of My Son (see 2 Corinthians 3:18).

Praying Scripture to Internalize Grace

Lord, there are times in my life when I am tempted to cry with Israel, "My way is hidden from the Lord; my cause is disregarded by my God" (Isaiah 40:27). During those seasons when I am hidden away from activity and affirmation, like the psalmist Asaph I wonder, "Will the Lord reject forever? Will he never show his favor again? Has his unfailing love vanished forever? . . . Has God forgotten to be merciful?" (Psalm 77:7-9). When I am tempted to think You have forgotten, help me to remember Your deeds and Your faithfulness—to remember Your miracles of long ago (see verse 11).

Help me to understand that it is for my own good that You often draw me into the place of obscurity. There in Your presence I have the opportunity to remember that I am not precious and priceless to You because I perform well but simply because You love and cherish me. Rather than questioning Your love, help me to trust Your unfailing love (see 13:5). Help me to meditate on Your unfailing love (see 48:9) and rejoice by faith that Your love for me is unchanging. Because of Your great love, I am not consumed, for Your compassions never fail; they are new every morning (see Lamentations 3:22-23). Help me sink into Your love during this time in the hidden place.

Holy Spirit, reshape me. Bring into my life the fruit of righteousness: love, joy, peace, patience, gentleness, and self-control (see Galatians 5:22). I pray that I would emerge from the hidden place transformed, less anxious to prove myself, less driven, less uptight and frazzled.

Thank You that I am "precious and honored in Your sight" (Isaiah 43:4). Your love for me is great, and Your faithfulness in loving me will continue into all eternity (see Psalm 117:2).

A Daily Dose of Grace

Day 1

1. Memorize and meditate on Colossians 3:1-3 as written here or in another translation:

   > You have been raised with Christ, set your hearts on things above, where Christ is seated at the right hand of God. Set your minds on things above, not on earthly things. For you died, and your life is now hidden with Christ in God.

2. In your own words, what does it mean to die to self?

3. Read Colossians 3:3 again. What security comes from knowing that your life is hidden away with Christ in God?

Day 2

1. Read John 12:20-26. What lessons does this parable teach us about grace?

2. Read Luke 9:23. What did Jesus mean when He invited us to take up our cross and follow Him?

3. Read Matthew 10:38-39. The Greek word for *life* that is used here is *psuche*. It refers to the soul, the total person, the self, which includes the personality with all its hopes and goals.[10] What does it mean to you personally to lose your life for the sake of Christ? In what ways do we find new life in Christ?

Day 3

1. Read James 4:6. How does God use the place of hiddenness (the place where activity, applause, and affirmation are absent) to form humility in our lives?

2. Read 1 Kings 17:19, 2 Kings 4:33, Mark 5:40, and Acts 9:40. Each of these miracles was performed in seclusion, without applause or affirmation from the crowd. Do you think God does His greatest and deepest works in seclusion? Why, or why not?

3. Read 1 Peter 1:6-7. How does God use the place of hiddenness to refine and purify us?

Day 4

1. Read Colossians 3:4. What does it mean to you that Christ is now your life?

2. Read Colossians 3:12. List each garment of grace. Next to each one, describe how your life reflects this quality.

3. Read Colossians 1:10. How does having Christ be your life increase your fruitfulness? What would increased fruitfulness look like in your life?

Day 5

1. Read 2 Corinthians 12:7-10. Paul experienced suffering and sorrow, which he pleaded for God to take away. God replied, "My grace is sufficient for you." How is God's grace sufficient in times of suffering and sorrow?

2. Read Galatians 2:20 and write a paraphrase of it. How does time in the hidden place help us more fully understand what it means to be crucified with Christ?

3. Read Galatians 2:20 again. When we die to self, Christ can then live His life through us without us getting in the way. Imagine that your hands are the hands of Christ, your feet the feet of Christ, your eyes the eyes of Christ, your ears the ears of Christ, and your tongue the tongue of Christ. How would that impact the way you live?

Day 6

1. Review Colossians 3:1-3. How has memorizing these verses impacted your life this week?

2. Have you ever spent time in the hidden place? Write a description of your experience. How has this chapter changed your perspective on that time?

3. It's possible that you are in the hidden place right now. You may even feel forgotten by God. In what tangible ways have you discovered that Christ's grace is sufficient? If Jesus were in the room with you, what do you think He would want to say to you?

SAY THANK YOU

Grace and gratitude belong together—like heaven and earth. Grace evokes gratitude like the voice an echo. Gratitude follows grace as thunder follows lightning.

KARL BARTH

When our eldest daughter, Bethany, was only two years old, we were living in Africa and she was exposed at an early age to many different cultures, one of those being British. I'll never forget when Bethany first heard a British friend say, "Thank you for the lovely dinner." Bethany was fascinated by the word *lovely* and so without much coaching used the word to thank a friend who had invited us for dinner. Our host was floored and made a big fuss that our two-year-old would say, "Thank you for the lovely dinner." Well, that was all the encouragement Bethany needed! From that moment on, our little people-pleasing toddler said the phrase as sweetly as possible to every person who hosted us. Was she genuinely thankful? Probably not, at two. But the more she said thank you, the more it became a habit.

As Bethany got a little older and people gave her gifts, she would jump up and down excitedly, saying thank you over and over again and occasionally throwing in the word *lovely* for effect. Though now an adult, Bethany is still effusive in her thanksgiving. In fact, I just got off the phone with her. She called to thank me for taking care of her son, Tyler, last night. As if it would ever be a burden to take care of my precious grandson!

God has given us an incredible gift: His grace. How can we offer anything less than effusive thanksgiving for this gift? Gratitude is the overflow of a grace-filled life. A story in Luke 7:36-50 demonstrates this principle.

A Dinner Party

In Jesus' day, roads in Palestine were dusty, and because most people walked everywhere, their feet were always filthy. When guests arrived at a dinner party, a servant would greet them and wash their feet. In addition, the host would greet guests at the door and kiss them on the cheek as a token of respect.

One day Simon the Pharisee invited Jesus to his home for a dinner party. However, when Jesus arrived, Simon's attitude spoke indifference rather than reverence or even respect. Simon's servants didn't wash Jesus' feet, nor did Simon greet Jesus with a kiss or anoint Him with oil, which was also the custom (see verse 45). Despite Simon's rudeness, Jesus entered the house and "reclined" at the table, as was the custom.[1] As the dinner progressed, an uninvited guest—a woman—entered. It's likely that most of the men in the room knew her, not because of her upstanding character in the community but because of the sexual services she offered. Some of them possibly had even visited her. Luke identifies the woman only as "a sinner." However, the unspoken is clear: She was not only a sinner, she was a notorious sinner.

She entered the room quietly. She had not come to eat; her hunger ran deeper than physical hunger. Her attention was fixed on Jesus. I imagine that a hush fell over the room as conversations stopped mid-sentence. The men watched in disbelief as she approached Jesus and knelt at His feet. Around her neck hung an expensive alabaster bottle of perfume. Alabaster was marble, and if it was pure, it was white or translucent.[2] Weeping softly, she let down her hair and took the lid off the bottle. The perfume she carried in the flask was both "aromatic and expensive."

The woman's weeping continued as she knelt before Jesus, pouring out her unexpected but costly offering on His feet. Perfume and tears flowed freely. Luke wrote that she "began to wet [Jesus'] feet with her tears" (verse 38). She went on to gently wipe His feet with the only towel she had: her beautiful long tresses of hair. Then she kissed His feet over and over again.

The onlookers sat in shocked silence, probably thinking, *Does He know? If He knew who she was, He would not let her kiss His feet like that. It's too sensual. It's embarrassing. Why doesn't He stop her?* This settled it for Simon. Jesus was not a prophet or surely He would have stopped this lavish and shameful display of affection from this woman (see verse 39). The moment that thought crossed Simon's mind, Jesus spoke: "Simon, I have something to tell you" (verse 40). The simple story Jesus told revealed to Simon that Jesus, the One whom he had decided was not a prophet, had just read his mind.

The story went like this. Two men owed money to a certain money-lender. One owed him five hundred denarii and the other fifty. Neither of them had the money to pay him back, so he canceled the debts of both.

Then Jesus asked Simon, "Now which of them will love [the moneylender] more?" (verse 42).

Simon knew at some internal level that he had been caught. I imagine he stammered a bit before answering, "I suppose the one who had the bigger debt canceled" (verse 43). He was likely thinking, *How did He know what I was thinking? Maybe He is a prophet after all!*

Jesus then reminded Simon that he, though righteous, had not been a gracious host. He had not provided any servant to wash Jesus' feet, had not kissed Jesus respectfully to greet Him, and had not anointed Him with olive oil. It's almost as if Jesus said to Simon, "Get over yourself! It's not about you and how righteous you are. Stop judging her worship." I wonder what would have happened if Jesus had said, "You know, Simon, you might try thanking me yourself sometime!"

The sinful woman had not stopped washing Jesus' feet with her tears; she had not stopped kissing Jesus' feet or pouring out her expensive perfume on them. She had been the recipient of love, cleansing, and forgiveness, and she felt that nothing was too good for the Lord, so she thanked Him in the most demonstrative way she could. Then Jesus said to Simon, "Her many sins have been forgiven—for she loved much. But he who has been forgiven little loves little" (verse 47).

GRACE GLIMPSE

Gratitude is the overflow of a grace-filled life.

The bottom line is this: God's extravagant grace calls for an exuberant response. That's the kind of response that delights God's heart.

Gratitude Delights God's Heart

God notices when we give Him thanks. In fact, more than merely noticing, He feels delighted. Check out Luke 17:11-19. You probably remember the story. Jesus was traveling to Jerusalem and along the way ten men with leprosy cried out to Him, "Jesus, Master, have pity on us!" (verse 13). People with leprosy were ostracized from society, so these men felt desperate. Jesus healed all ten of them and instructed them to go and show themselves to the priest so they could be declared healed and rejoin society. The ten went off excitedly, and one turned around and ran back to Jesus to say thank you. The Bible tells us that he fell at the feet of Jesus and thanked Him. Jesus definitely noticed. He said,

"Were not all ten cleansed? Where are the other nine?" (verse 17). He was asking, "Are you the only one who came back to give thanks?"

God blesses those who give Him thanks. Check out these passages:

> May the peoples praise you, O God; may all the peoples praise you. Then the land will yield its harvest, and God, our God, will bless us. (Psalm 67:5-6)

> About midnight Paul and Silas were praying and singing hymns to God [in other words—they were thanking God]. . . . Suddenly there was such a violent earthquake that the foundations of the prison were shaken. At once all the prison doors flew open, and everybody's chains came loose. (Acts 16:25-26)

When we thank God in all circumstances, God blesses us by loosing the chains that bind us. Not only does gratitude delight God's heart, it also transforms us.

Gratitude Transforms Us

As I've thought about how gratitude transforms us, several ideas have come to mind.

Gratitude soothes anxiety. Most performers carry quite a bit of anxiety—anxiety over how they measure up, about whether they are getting ahead or managing their schedule. Their anxiety leaves them feeling worried and exhausted. This is why Paul wrote, "Do not be anxious about anything, but in everything, by prayer and petition, with thanksgiving, present your requests to God" (Philippians 4:6). Thanksgiving is the antidote to anxiety.

I have certainly found this to be true in my life. When anxiety keeps me up or bombards my thoughts, I have learned to give thanks. I thank the Lord, by faith, that I can trust His grace. I thank Him that He loves me and knows what is going on in my world. I thank Him that He will empower me to meet whatever challenges lie ahead. I thank Him that His love will never fail me, even if others feel disappointed in me. As I thank Him, my anxious thoughts are calmed and I am able to rest assured that His grace is sufficient.

Gratitude quiets the urge to judge. When we are consumed with thanking God for His grace in our lives, we don't waste our time evaluating others. On the other hand, when we feel indifferent about God's grace, it's easy to judge others.

It's my conviction that the tendency to judge the thanksgiving of others is dividing the American church today. Isn't it interesting how worship, which is supposed to be about offering thanksgiving to God, has become something over which we fight? Many in the American church have come to the faulty conclusion that worship on Sunday morning is to be a show designed to serve their own preferences. I don't mean to sound harsh, but worship was never meant to be about us; it's about God. Rather than evaluating the worship music at our churches, let's focus on offering God effusive thanks for His grace. I'm guessing that the tendency to judge how others worship will diminish.

Gratitude increases your kindness factor. I know that sounds simple, but it is the truth. The world can be a harsh, unforgiving place. In their efforts to get to the top, many performers step over or use people without even realizing it. However, the more we cultivate an attitude of gratitude, the kinder we will treat others. The more we come before God with thanksgiving, the more His Spirit seems to tenderize our hearts toward others. As a result, we're just plain nicer!

Gratitude strengthens you to cope with stress. If I thank the Lord that He is in control of my life, when stress comes, the Holy Spirit replaces the tension in my soul with calm. When I choose to thank Him above the chaos of my life, the Holy Spirit quiets those feelings of being overwhelmed and I experience His rest. He brings calm to the most intense moments of life.

My friend Jill has experienced this as well. She is an executive assistant to the president of a large engineering firm. Not only does Jill have a demanding job, her mom is in a nursing home with Parkinson's and dementia. Jill tries to visit nearly every day, she checks in with her dad, and she and her husband, Greg, lead a small-group Bible study. Jill could be completely stressed out, but most days when I talk to her, she exudes a calm that can come only from the Holy Spirit. It is because long ago, as a child, Jill learned the power of praising God. She lives a lifestyle of thanksgiving every day. She says,

> At the onset of my relationship with Christ, my brother instilled in me a heart for worship and thanksgiving, and I would have to say it is my deepest connection with my Father. It has been both a necessity and a delight as I walk daily with Him. I praise Him through Scripture, through the alphabet, focusing on his attributes, through song, through the "I am" statements, through thankfulness. I have truly experienced the benefit of filling my heart with praise and thanksgiving as I walk through the blessings and trials of each day. Worshipping Him has set me free from a driven lifestyle. While the stress could overwhelm me, as I thank Him He pours calm into my life and He is magnified.

Gratitude curbs the tendency to complain. Remember the Israelites? God rescued them from Egypt and orchestrated a miraculous deliverance for them. But it was not enough. No matter how God provided for them, they complained. Because of this, the Lord did not allow the original generation that escaped from Egypt, except for Joshua and Caleb, to enter the Promised Land. These two men were the only ones who felt gratitude to God for the land He was providing and trusted Him to take them into that land safely (see Numbers 14:1-38).

While traveling in Israel, I visited the Sinai Desert, where the Israelites wandered for forty years because of their complaining. As I looked around, the Spirit of God pierced my heart and I made a renewed commitment to give Him thanks for His grace in my life rather than complain. As a reminder, I picked up a small stone and brought it home. It sits on my bedroom dresser to remind me to give thanks. The more I give thanks, the less I complain.

Gratitude opens our hearts to experience God's grace more deeply. This is as it should be. In the Old Testament, God said He wanted to have first place in our hearts (see Exodus 20:3). Though we don't like to admit it, when we are in performance mode, we are very self-focused. Gratitude lifts our attention off ourselves and our problems and onto the only One powerful enough to solve them. The more I thanked God for His grace, the less concerned I was about how others perceived me. I felt so thankful for His love and forgiveness that if others didn't approve of me, it was okay because I knew God approved of me. My thoughts changed from who didn't love me to who did love me. And the One who loved me offered me perfect love 24/7.

My friend Linda also experienced this. She began to "enter his gates with thanksgiving" (Psalm 100:4) and describes how her experience of God's grace deepened:

> Often the One I loved would wake me in the night, and I would get up and trust my sleep to Him. I yearned to be with Him, to "hang out" with Him, and to bask in His presence as my father, friend, and lover.[3]

Gratitude defeats the Enemy. Satan would love nothing more than to see you return to the bondage of performance. He will try every angle to rob you from internalizing the freedom that is yours through God's grace. So it's important to have a plan. I find that if I faithfully thank the Lord, especially using portions of Scripture, then Satan is defeated and I am able to stand firm in my new freedom.

In the Old Testament, there is a story about King Jehoshaphat that

I simply love (see 2 Chronicles 20). Jehoshaphat was leading his army into battle, and the people felt afraid because it seemed slaughter was imminent. Then the king gave a rather strange command. He appointed people to sing and offer thanksgiving to God in front of the army as they went out to battle. Rather than cowering in fear, the choir began to march out in front, singing, "Give thanks to the Lord, for his love endures forever" (verse 21). As their praise rose up to the heavens, the Lord sent an ambush against their enemies.

If you long to be free from old, toxic messages, start thanking God for His grace when they pop into your mind. When we choose to thank God by faith in spite of our circumstances, the Enemy is defeated! As we offer praise, God will do extraordinary things on our behalf.

Author and worship leader Darlene Zschech wrote, "Praise is a declaration, a victory cry, proclaiming faith to stand firm in the place God has given you. Praise is a proclamation that the enemy's intent to plunder you will not rock you. Praise declares that you will not be moved by the enemy's attempt to snatch you away."[4]

Effusive Thanksgiving

I want to be effusive in my thanksgiving, don't you? Someday we will be offering thanksgiving 24/7 to the Grace Giver. We won't need to remind ourselves; it will come naturally. Our hearts will be overwhelmed with the depth of His grace. We will be face-to-face with the One who knows, loves, forgives, empowers, and pursues us for all eternity. Until then, this is just our dress rehearsal. I want to practice intentionally now for the genuine, heart-felt concert we will give then. Will you join me?

Message from the Grace Giver

My child, someday you will join Me in heaven, and together with people and tribes from every nation, tribe, and tongue, you will sing, "To him who sits on the throne and to the Lamb be praise and honor and glory and power, for ever and ever" (Revelation 5:13). Your thanksgiving and worship now is practice for then. Come and praise Me. As you thank Me, you will experience My presence as never before. I inhabit the praises of My people (see Psalm 22:3). Throw away any inhibition and allow My Spirit to awaken your soul to the ecstatic joy of My presence. Exuberantly give Me thanks. Let Me show you how much I love you. There in My presence, the opinions of others will not matter. You will be consumed with only Me.

PRAYING SCRIPTURE TO INTERNALIZE GRACE

Hallelujah! Salvation and glory and power belong to our God, for true and just are His judgments (see Revelation 19:1). Thank You, Holy One, for inviting me to worship You. In Your presence, I am set free. Be exalted, O Lord! Great and marvelous are Your deeds. Just and true are Your ways, King of the Ages (see 15:3). "Worthy is the Lamb, who was slain, to receive power and wealth and wisdom and strength and honor and glory and praise! . . . To him who sits on the throne and to the Lamb be praise and honor and glory and power, for ever and ever!" (5:12-13). Lord Jesus, Lamb of God, what a privilege to worship You and give You thanks!

Praise the Lord, O my soul. All my inmost being, praise His holy name. Praise the Lord, O my soul, and forget not He who forgives all my sin and heals all my diseases and who redeems my life from the pit and crowns me with love and compassion (see Psalm 103:1-4). Awaken my heart to worship You continuously. Fill my mouth with Your thanksgiving as I move throughout my day.

Lord Jesus, I long to continually offer You a sacrifice of thanksgiving. You have offered me such extravagant grace, and in return I want to offer You extravagant thanksgiving and worship. You are great and worthy of praise. You are exalted far above all gods (see 96:4). My soul is filled with so much thanksgiving to You. I bow before You and extol You with music and singing (see 95:2). I rejoice in You, Lord. I praise Your holy name. I will sing to You, for You have done marvelous things both in my life and in the lives of others (see 98:1). I will enter Your gates with thanksgiving and Your courts with praise; I will give thanks to You and praise Your name, for You are good, and Your love endures forever, and Your faithfulness continues through all generations (see 100:4-5). O, Lord my God, You are very great; You are clothed with splendor and majesty (see 104:1).

What a privilege to worship You and give You thanks. You alone are worthy of all of my praise.

A Daily Dose of Grace

Day 1

1. Memorize and meditate on Psalm 106:1 as written here or in another translation:

    > Praise the Lord. Give thanks to the Lord, for he is good; his love endures forever. Who can proclaim the mighty acts of the Lord or fully declare his praise?

2. What keeps you from giving thanks on a regular basis? What would it look like for you to become more intentional about praising and thanking God for His grace?

3. How does your life "proclaim" God's grace?

Day 2

1. Read Luke 7:36-50. Imagine that you are attending the dinner at Simon's house. Describe the atmosphere in the room: what you see, hear, smell, and feel as the sinful woman worships Jesus.

2. Describe the sinful woman's worship. How does it demonstrate effusiveness?

3. Describe Simon's attitude.

4. Are you more like Simon or the sinful woman in the way you give thanks?

5. Think back to the story Jesus told. How do you think brokenness affects our gratitude for God's grace?

Day 3

1. Read Psalm 136. How many times does the psalmist write, "His love endures forever"?

2. What does it mean to you personally that His love endures forever?

3. Write your own psalm of thanksgiving for the Lord's unfailing love. In your psalm, list the ways the Lord has demonstrated His love toward you personally.

Day 4

1. Read Luke 17:11-19. How many lepers asked Jesus to have pity on them? How many returned to give thanks?

2. Describe the one leper's thanksgiving. How is it similar to the sinful woman's thanksgiving?

3. Describe Jesus' response to the one leper's gratitude. What does this teach us about how God feels about our gratitude?

4. Jesus said to the one thankful leper, "Your faith has made you well" (verse 19). All the lepers were healed of leprosy. What do you think Jesus had in mind when He singled out this one leper and told him that his faith had made him well? It seems to me he experienced more than merely physical healing—what do you think?

Day 5

1. Read 2 Samuel 6:16-22. This story describes David's excitement and thanksgiving when the ark of the Lord was brought back into Jerusalem.

   a. Describe David's thanksgiving.

b. How did his wife Michal respond?

c. How is Michal's attitude similar to Simon's in Luke 7?

d. How does internalizing God's grace make us less judgmental of how others give thanks and worship?

Day 6

1. Review Psalm 106:1.

2. Grace tells you that you are completely known, loved, forgiven, empowered, and pursued by God. Take each of those principles and write a prayer expressing your thanksgiving to the Lord.

   Example:
   Known: "Lord Jesus, thank You that You know me completely. I don't need my false self anymore. Thank You that I don't ever need to hide from You."

Loved:

Forgiven:

Empowered:

Pursued:

3. Read each of these passages and then write a prayer of thanksgiving. (You don't have to use every verse or all of every verse. Use just the ones that speak to you.)
   a. Psalm 148:13

   b. Psalm 150:1-2

c. Ephesians 1:7

d. Ephesians 2:5-9

LIVE IN THE SPIRIT

Fix your desire upon this divine, wondrous grace: "I will dwell in them."

ANDREW MURRAY

It's been quite a journey, hasn't it? I'm glad we've been in it together! Thank you for joining me and allowing me to share my heart with you. I have been praying for you throughout our study, and my prayer for you continues. May you continue to stand firm in the freedom you have experienced.

If you take away only one truth from this book, I pray it is this: You can be free from performing only because the Holy Spirit dwells in you. Did you get that? *The living God dwells in you!* You don't have to try harder; you only have to move out of the way and allow Him to live through you. Only through His indwelling power can you experience God's grace. Rather than setting your desire on a "more successful" Christian walk, set your desire on the filling of the Holy Spirit moment by moment.

BEING FILLED WITH THE SPIRIT

To be filled with the Spirit does not mean we have more of the Holy Spirit in our lives at any given moment. It means we surrender more of ourselves to Him. When we are filled with the Holy Spirit, He consumes us and we are completely controlled by Him (see Ephesians 5:17-18). Then and only then will His fruit flow out of our lives.

Although the Holy Spirit comes to dwell in us the moment we receive Christ and His grace, we are called to be *continually* filled with the Spirit. To be continually filled means we will be filled over and over again. The filling of the Spirit is not a onetime event. This is where many believers become confused. In the book of Acts, we see at least three different occasions where Peter was filled with the Spirit (see 2:4; 4:8,31).

R. A. Torrey, an evangelist and Bible scholar, played a part in some of the greatest revivals in history. Writing about the Holy Spirit, Torrey said, "Repeated fillings with the Holy Spirit are necessary to continuance and increase of power."[1] Torrey is not talking about power to prove we are valuable; he is talking about power to live the grace walk victoriously. Through the filling of the Holy Spirit, we gain victory, boldness, power, passion, and the strength to not go back to the life of the performer.

The bottom line is that we cannot live the grace walk alone. It is a Spirit walk. Paul wrote, "Since we live by the Spirit, let us keep in step with the Spirit" (Galatians 5:25).

Allow the Holy Spirit to Take the Lead

I have always wanted to be "the leader." I remember that even as a young child, teachers acknowledged leadership skills in me. Those words of affirmation made me want to prove even more that I was a leader. But when it comes to keeping step with the Spirit, leadership skills are not always what's best. In the dance of life, there can only be *one* leader. That one leader must be the Holy Spirit. If I fight Him, trying to be the leader, the dance will not go well. Rather than keeping in step with Him, I end up stepping on His toes. Instead of flowing with Him, I end up grieving Him (see Ephesians 4:30). How can I tell if I've taken the lead? Here are a few telltale signs:

- I try to figure out problems in my own strength.
- I feel tense and stressed out.
- I feel afraid rather than courageous.
- I run back to my pseudo-self in an effort to look better.

So because the pull for every performer is to return to the life of performance, I have begun to acknowledge at the onset of every day, *Holy Spirit, You are leading the dance today. Bring my steps into union with Yours. Help me dance as one with You.*

LISTEN FOR HIS VOICE THROUGHOUT THE DAY

When I do this, I am reminded that this life is not about how well I perform or how much I accomplish; it's about allowing the Holy Spirit to live His life through me.

How do I cultivate this awareness? I check in with Him throughout the day. When I feel baffled by a problem, I whisper, "Holy Spirit, help. Please lead me into all truth and wisdom as You have promised" (see John 16:13). The more I cultivate a sense of His presence, the more sensitive I am to His voice. He may speak to me through His Word or through the soft whisper of His voice deep within my spirit. If I am cruising through life, not attentive to His voice, I might not yield when He convicts me of an attitude or action not in alignment with His desires for my life. In those moments, rather than admitting I am wrong, I grab one of my old masks in an attempt to make myself look better. Knowing this, I intentionally work to cultivate a continual awareness of His presence.

REPENT WHEN YOU GRIEVE HIM

More than anything, I want to live a Spirit-filled life, but in spite of my good intentions, sometimes I step on His toes. Just this morning in a phone conversation with someone close to me, I spoke too soon, too strong, and too much. I knew afterward that I had grieved the Holy Spirit, because He brought conviction that I need to listen before speaking. Otherwise, how can I hear Him whisper? He also pointed out that I don't need to always give my opinion, even if I feel my opinion is valid. So I told the Holy Spirit how sorry I was for trying to lead the dance and stepping on His toes. I asked Him to forgive me. I also called the woman with whom I had been speaking, apologized, and asked her to forgive me as well. I then told the Holy Spirit that I wanted to get back in the dance and that I was more than willing for Him to lead.

Living life in the fullness of the Spirit is the most amazing way to experience God's presence every day. It takes all the pressure off of us to perform. Instead, we can enjoy freedom even in a world that applauds performance. I invite you to pray the following prayer, asking the Holy Spirit to fill you with Himself. Allow Him to lead the dance, and you will experience more freedom than you have ever known before.

> Dear Lord Jesus, I realize I have lived so much of my Christian life as though it were a self-improvement course, continually trying harder. Forgive me, Lord, for trying to do it in my own strength. Thank You for leaving Your Spirit to indwell and empower me.
>
> Holy Spirit, please come now and fill me. I long for more of Your power and presence in my life. Take over my whole life. Control my thoughts, feelings, and activities. Live Your life through me. Show me what's important and what's not. Direct me on when to say yes and when to say no. Flow through me with Your love as I live in relationship with others. Love them through me. Convict me when I grieve You. Increase my sensitivity to You. I don't want to live this Christian life in my own strength, so I ask You to enable me to live in sync with You. Bring my will into perfect union with Yours.

A DAILY DOSE OF GRACE

Day 1

1. Memorize and meditate on Galatians 5:25 as written here or in another translation:

   > Since we live by the Spirit, let us keep in step with the Spirit.

2. Read Ephesians 5:18. In your own words, describe what it means to be filled with the Holy Spirit.

3. If you were filled with the Holy Spirit, how would your life look?

Day 2

1. Read Acts 2:4, 4:8, and 4:31. Describe what happened to Peter when he was "filled with the Holy Spirit."

2. How is the filling of the Spirit evidence of God's grace?

3. Read Acts 1:8. What does this Scripture teach us about being filled with the Holy Spirit?

4. How does the filling of the Spirit transform us?

5. What is our part in that transformation?

Day 3

1. Read John 15:1-4. Are we to work harder to achieve these character traits? Please explain.

2. What correlation is there between abiding and being filled with the Holy Spirit?

3. Read John 16:7. Why do you think Jesus said it was better that He go away and that the Holy Spirit come?

4. Read John 14:16-18. What promise does Jesus give here about the Holy Spirit? Did He keep His promise?

5. How does the Holy Spirit help us not to live as orphans?

Day 4

1. Read Galatians 5:22-23. Describe the growth that happens in our lives when we are filled with the Holy Spirit.

2. What correlation is there between being filled with the Spirit and standing firm in our freedom?

3. Read Galatians 5:25. What tangible steps can you take to keep step with the Spirit?

4. In what ways can you cultivate a continual sense of the Holy Spirit's presence in your life?

Day 5

1. Read Romans 8:5-6. Describe the differences between the mind controlled by the flesh and the mind controlled by the Spirit.

2. Read Romans 8:11. How does the Holy Spirit empower us to do the things we might otherwise not be able to do?

3. Read Romans 8:16. How does the Spirit reassure us that we belong to God?

4. Read Romans 8:26-27. How does the Holy Spirit help us in our weakness? How does He help us when we pray?

Day 6

1. Review Galatians 5:25.

2. What new lessons did you learn about yourself during this study?

3. What did you learn about God?

4. How have you experienced more freedom from having done this study?

5. Look over the prayer to be filled with the Holy Spirit. Are you ready to take this step? Why, or why not?

NOTES

CHAPTER 1: BORN TO PERFORM

1. Joanna Weaver, *Having a Mary Heart in a Martha World* (Colorado Springs, CO: Waterbrook, 2000), 66.
2. David Seamands, *Healing Grace* (Indianapolis: Light and Life Communications, 1999), 121.
3. W. E. Vine, *An Expository Dictionary of New Testament Words* (Old Tappan, NJ: Revell, 1966), 170.
4. Herbert Lockyer, *All the Parables of the Bible* (Grand Rapids, MI: Zondervan, 1963), 12.
5. James Montgomery Boice, *The Parables of Jesus* (Chicago: Moody, 1983), 10.

CHAPTER 2: FIND FREEDOM FROM SHAME

1. Herbert Lockyer *All the Parables of the Bible* (Grand Rapids, MI: Zondervan, 1963), 231.
2. Earl R. Henslin, PsyD, *The Way Out of the Wilderness* (Nashville: Thomas Nelson, 1991), 81.
3. Cynthia Spell Humbert, *Deceived by Shame, Desired by God* (Colorado Springs, CO: NavPress, 2001), 22.
4. David Seamands, *Healing Grace* (Indianapolis: Light and Life Communications, 1999), 155.
5. Robert S. McGee, *The Search for Significance* (Houston: Rapha Publishing, 1990), 337.
6. Beth Moore, *Breaking Free* (Nashville: LifeWay, 1999), 121.
7. W. E. Vine, *An Expository Dictionary of New Testament Words* (Old Tappan, NJ: Revell, 1966), 133.

8. Paul E. Billheimer, *Destined for the Throne* (Minneapolis: Bethany, 1975), 120–121.

Chapter 3: Build a Rock-Solid Core

1. Adele Ahlberg, *Calhoun Spiritual Disciplines Handbook* (Downers Grove, IL: InterVarsity, 2005), 290, glossary.
2. Robert S. McGee, *The Search for Significance* (Houston: Rapha Publishing, 1990), 27.
3. Bruce B. Barton, Linda K. Taylor, and David R. Veerman, *Life Application Bible Commentary: Luke* (Wheaton, IL: Tyndale, 1997), 168.
4. Nancie Carmichael, *The Comforting Presence of God* (Eugene, OR: Harvest House, 2004), 35.

Chapter 4: Give Yourself Permission to Rest

1. Charles Swindoll, *The Greatest Life of All Jesus* (Nashville: Thomas Nelson, 2008), 87.
2. W. E. Vine, *An Expository Dictionary of New Testament Words* (Old Tappan, NJ: Revell, 1966), 287.
3. Rob Bell, *Velvet Elvis* (Grand Rapids, MI: Zondervan, 2005), 47, 126–129.
4. Nancie Carmichael, *The Comforting Presence of God* (Eugene, OR: Harvest House, 2004), 26.
5. Ron Hall and Denver Moore with Lynn Vincent, *Same Kind of Different as Me* (Nashville: Thomas Nelson, 2006), 109.
6. Judith Hougen, *Transformed into Fire* (Grand Rapids, MI: Kregel, 2002), 173.
7. Hougen, 173.
8. Jeanne Guyon, *Experiencing the Depths of Jesus Christ* (Gardiner, ME: Christian Books Publishing House, 1981), 53.
9. Isaac Penington, "Waiting for Breathings from His Spirit," in *Devotional Classics*, eds. Richard J. Foster and James Bryan Smith (San Francisco: HarperSanFrancisco, 1990, 2005), 207.

Chapter 5: Find Your Purpose and Passion

1. Rick Warren, *The Purpose-Driven Life* (Grand Rapids, MI: Zondervan, 2002), 17.

2. Jean Fleming, *Finding Focus in a Whirlwind World* (Fort Collins, CO: Treasure!, 1991), 24.
3. Mother Teresa, *A Message of Love to the World*, http://living.oneindia.n/celebrity/other-celebrities/mother.teresa.biography.htm.

CHAPTER 6: PUT AWAY THE MEASURING STICK

1. Bruce B. Barton, Mark Fackler, Linda K. Taylor, and David R. Veerman, *Life Application Bible Commentary: Matthew* (Wheaton, IL: Tyndale, 1996), 387.
2. *Merriam-Webster's Collegiate Dictionary*, 10th ed., s.v. "envy."
3. W. E. Vine, *An Expository Dictionary of New Testament Words* (Old Tappan, NJ: Revell, 1966), 37.
4. John Bunyan, quoted in Richard J. Foster and James Bryan Smith, eds., *Devotional Classics* (San Francisco: HarperSanFrancisco, 1993), 217.
5. Thomas Merton, *Thoughts on Solitude* (New York: Farrar Straus & Giroux, 1989), 41–42.
6. William Law, quoted in R. T. Kendall, *Just Say Thanks* (Lake Mary, FL: Charisma House, 2005), 37.

CHAPTER 7: LET GO OF BEING PERFECT

1. *NIV Thinline Reference Bible* (Grand Rapids, MI: Zondervan, 1984), 1107, study note at the bottom of the page.
2. W. E. Vine, *An Expository Dictionary of New Testament Words* (Old Tappan, NJ: Revell, 1940), 72.
3. Bruce B. Barton, Mark Fackler, Linda K. Taylor, and David R. Veerman, *Life Application Bible Commentary: Philippians, Colossians, Philemon* (Wheaton, IL: Tyndale, 1996), 225.
4. Beth Moore, *Praying God's Word* (Nashville: Broadman, Holman, 2000), 57.

CHAPTER 8: DISCOVER YOUR TRUE BELOVEDNESS

1. Kenneth E. Bailey, *The Cross and the Prodigal* (Downers Grove, IL: InterVarsity, 2005), 53–54.
2. Bailey, 59.
3. Bailey, 52.
4. Bailey, 67.
5. Bailey, 68.

CHAPTER 9: WALK AWAY FROM THE BAIT

1. Bruce B. Barton, Mark Fackler, Linda K. Taylor, and David R. Veerman, *Life Application Bible Commentary: Matthew* (Wheaton, IL: Tyndale, 1996), 363.
2. This parable does not teach that your acceptance with God is conditional on how well you offer grace to others. If that were the case, your acceptance with God would be based not only on grace but also works. Ephesians 2:8-9 clearly teaches us that our salvation is completely by grace and not as the result of works. Further, if our salvation and acceptance with God was based on how well we forgave others, none of us would be accepted or saved. Even the most gracious believers struggle with offering forgiveness.
3. Becky Harling, *Rewriting Your Emotional Script* (Colorado Springs, CO: NavPress, 2008), 171.
4. W. E. Vine, *An Expository Dictionary of New Testament Words* (Old Tappan, NJ: Revell, 1940), 131.

CHAPTER 10: SURRENDER IN THE HIDDEN PLACE

1. Used with permission.
2. Henri Nouwen, Henri Nouwen Society, email_lists@henrinouwen.org, Daily Meditation for August 14, 2008.
3. Catherine Hart Weber. These words were written to me in a personal e-mail.
4. Joni Eareckson Tada, "Borrowing God's Smile," *Discipleship Journal* 167 (September/October 2008): 37.
5. Henri Nouwen, *The Inner Voice of Love: A Journey Through Anguish to Freedom* (New York: Doubleday, 1996), 21.
6. Ruth Myers with Warren Myers, *31 Days of Praise* (Sisters, OR: Multnomah, 1994), 127.
7. Andrew Murray, *Humility* (Gainesville, FL: Bridge-Logos Publishers, 2000), vii.
8. Bruce B. Barton, Mark Fackler, Linda K. Taylor, and David R. Veerman, *Life Application Bible Commentary: John* (Wheaton, IL: Tyndale, 1995), 216.
9. Brennan Manning, *Abba's Child* (Colorado Springs, CO: NavPress, 1994), 151.

10. Bruce B. Barton, Mark Fackler, Linda K. Taylor, and David R. Veerman, *Life Application Bible Commentary: Matthew* (Wheaton, IL: Tyndale, 1996), 215.

CHAPTER 11: SAY THANK YOU

1. Bruce B. Barton, Linda K. Taylor, and David R. Veerman, *Life Application Bible Commentary: Luke* (Wheaton, IL: Tyndale, 1997), 189.
2. Merrill C. Tenney, ed., *The Zondervan Pictorial Encyclopedia of the Bible, Volume 1* (Grand Rapids, MI: Zondervan, 1976), 95.
3. Linda Dillow, *Satisfy My Thirsty Soul* (Colorado Springs, CO: NavPress, 2007), 45.
4. Darlene Zschech, quoted in Stormie Omartian, *The Prayer That Changes Everything* (Eugene, OR: Harvest House, 2004), 205.

CHAPTER 12: LIVE IN THE SPIRIT

1. R. A. Torrey, *Holy Spirit* (Lynnwood, WA: Emerald Books, 1998), 93.

About the Author

Becky Harling is a frequent speaker at women's conferences and retreats nationally as well as internationally. She is the author of *Finding Calm in Life's Chaos* and *Rewriting Your Emotional Script*. Drawing from her experiences as a pastor's wife, mother, and breast cancer survivor, Becky delivers a message of hope and healing to women that is refreshingly transparent. Her husband, Steve, is the lead pastor at Foothills Community Church in Arvada, Colorado. Steve and Becky have four grown children and two grandchildren. To stay in touch with Becky, schedule her for your event, or learn more about her ministry, visit www.beckyharling.com.